# Table of Contents

# Acknowledgements

This book has been a long time in coming. I know there are many who are glad to see me stop talking about it and actually get it done! Here are three who had more patience with me than most:

**Bonnie Grau,** who helped me get the idea off the ground. Only you and I know, Bonnie, just how much of the first chapter is your creative work.

**Shirley Brosius,** who combined her editing skills, her gift of encouragement, and her talent as a teacher to guide me through completing the book as a graduate research project.

And last but not least, my wife, **Jacque,** who was always there to cheer me on when the going got tough. Now you won't have to hear, "Hey, listen to this paragraph!" anymore—at least, not until my next writing project!

David E. Fessenden

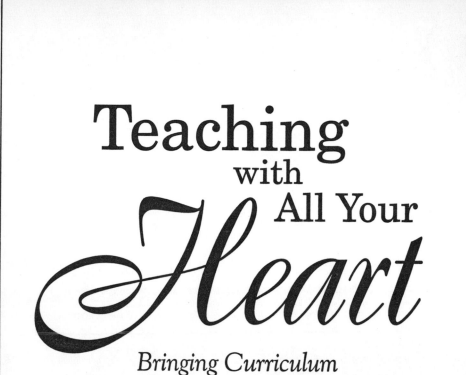

# Teaching
## with
## All Your
# *Heart*

*Bringing Curriculum*
*& Class to Life*

Cook

DAVID E. FESSENDEN

Cook Communications Ministries, Colorado Springs, Colorado 80918
Cook Communications, Paris, Ontario
Kingsway Communications, Eastbourne, England

TEACHING WITH ALL YOUR HEART
© 2002 by David E. Fessenden

First Printing, 2002
Printed in the United States of America

1 2 3 4 5 6 7 8 9 10 Printing/Year 06 05 04 03 02

Editor: Cheryl Crews
Cover Design: BMB Design, Inc.

Library of Congress Cataloging-in-Publication Data

Fessenden, David E.
Teaching with all your heart : bringing curriculum & class to life /
David E. Fessenden.
p. cm.
Includes bibliographical references (p.      ).
ISBN 0-7814-4913-8
1. Christian education--Teaching methods.  I. Title.
BV1534 .F47 2002
268'.6--dc21
2002008714

# Introduction

T HE CROWD IS HUSHED AS "THE GREAT ZAMBEEZIE" STEPS ONTO THE HIGH WIRE.

*What a time to get stage fright,* thinks "The Great Zambeezie," whose real name is Irving Kerplotz. *I've done it thousands of times during practice, but here—in front of the crowd—my legs are rubbery, my palms are sweaty, and my mind is a blank.*

Ever feel this way just before teaching a Sunday school class? Unlike "The Great Zambeezie," though, you do have a tool that acts as a harness, a net, and keeps the wire only inches from the ground: the word-for-word "screenplay" of your trusty teacher's manual. Sometimes you cling to it like a life preserver as you step in front of your class. If you ever get stuck in your presentation, you can always refer to the scripted monologue to keep you on track.

---

**This step can lead to a method of teaching that capitalizes on your creativity, highlights your spiritual gifts, and gives you the confidence to stand**

before a Sunday school class without the teacher's guide clutched in your white-knuckled, trembling hands. It is teaching with all your heart.

_____

If you're reading this book, it probably means you've grown tired of that scenario, and you're wondering if there's a different way to teach. If so, I congratulate you. This step can lead to a method of teaching that capitalizes on your creativity, highlights your spiritual gifts, and gives you confidence to stand before a Sunday school class without the teacher's guide clutched in your white-knuckled, trembling hands. It is "teaching with all your heart."

This doesn't mean you will throw out your Sunday school material. On the contrary, you will begin to use it more effectively because you will use it as it is intended by the publisher. *Teaching with All Your Heart* shows you how to customize your curriculum to fit your own unique teaching style and the particular needs of your students.

Sunday school teachers come in all shapes and sizes, and they approach their lessons with a variety of teaching styles and degrees of preparation. Likewise, there is an abundance of excellent Sunday school curriculum on the market. But must that material be followed verbatim? Can it be adapted to your unique situation? If so, how?

This book attempts to answer these questions. The goal of *Teaching with All Your Heart* is to show teachers how to customize their lessons, both for their students and to a style that is comfortable for them. But before we do that, I'd like to introduce you to a few Sunday school teachers. They may seem vaguely familiar; perhaps one of them is a little like you.

## ROGER'S STORY

There was a real problem with the first grade boys' Sunday school class in Pastor Betzer's church. The class had always had women teachers, many who had resigned in tears. Eventually, it had become impossible to get teachers for the group.

One Sunday morning while Dr. Betzer was preaching, he noticed Roger, a farmer who was about 30, sitting partway back in the church. At the same instant, he felt God telling him to ask Roger to teach that first grade class.

Dr. Betzer began arguing with God—even as he was preaching—for Roger was a most unlikely candidate for the job. He was shy, didn't make eye contact during conversations, and talked under his breath. Nevertheless, at the close of the service, Dr. Betzer arranged to talk to Roger.

When they met the next day, the pastor wasted no time in getting to the point. Much to his surprise, Roger looked straight at him and accepted the position.

Four times in the next four months, Roger's class had to be moved to larger quarters. It was not unusual to see children waving to him in his car Sunday mornings calling, "Goodbye, Roger. We love you!"

When Dr. Betzer could no longer contain his curiosity, he decided to visit Roger's class. The first thing he noticed as he approached the room was that all of the chairs were stacked in the hallway. Then he heard the baaing of a sheep. Cracking the door and peeping in, he saw dozens of little boys sitting cross-legged on the floor with open Bibles in their laps, staring attentively at Roger. Walking around the room were four big, live, smelly sheep.

And Roger? He was sitting in the corner of the room holding an open Bible and a little lamb and teaching about the Good Shepherd.[1]

Not many of us would be able to teach a class this way; many of us would not even want to! But Roger taught his class out of his own experience—and what was dear to his heart. He was a farmer, and he knew that Jesus' parables would make more sense if his students had a special type of visual aid—which just happened to be at his disposal.

It's unlikely that Roger's teacher's manual suggested that he bring live sheep to class—but there was probably something in the curriculum that sparked this unique idea for him. Roger customized his curriculum and adapted the material for his situation. And that ability to adapt, along with a healthy love for his students, made him an effective teacher.

## FREE-WHEELING BUT FRUSTRATED

Joe had a whirlwind week, and now, late on Saturday night, he barely has any time to get ready for his Sunday school class. He knows he's not at his best on Saturday evening, but the terrifying thought of standing in front of his students without having prepared keeps him going.

As he scans the teacher's guide he feels a vague sense of guilt, but he manages to push it into the background. *After all, he reasons to himself, I'm a busy guy. Those teaching seminars and articles that call for hours of preparation are just unrealistic.*

Deep down, however, he knows he's making excuses. The real problem is that he doesn't know how to prepare. All his attempts to teach a class the "proper" way have ended in failure. Besides, there's a certain excitement in "winging it." Many of his more off-the-cuff teaching experiences have been very well-received. There's a freshness and spontaneity when he improvises.

Of course, his approach to teaching also has its awkward moments—times when he loses his way, and panic sets in. That's when he wishes he had prepared more thoroughly. But then, that's what the teacher's guide is for, isn't it? When his lesson hits a rough spot, he just checks the script to see where to go next.

## PREPARED BUT PERPLEXED

Unlike Joe, Mary is the consummate preparer. She begins on Sunday afternoon with a detailed review of the teacher's guide. Each evening of the week, she spends 30-40 minutes in further study; every Scripture is referenced and read, sometimes even memorized. The other teachers admire her dedication and organization.

Still, Mary can't seem to shake the feeling that something's wrong. No matter how much she prepares, the class never goes according to plan. Someone always asks a question at the wrong time, upsetting the perfectly balanced outline of the lesson. And there's no time to deal with student questions anyway. If she does, she can't cover every last bit of material in the teacher's guide—and that's the main goal, isn't it?

Mary isn't blind to what is happening; she knows that the more energetic students are stifled, and the shy ones aren't participating. And she hates being so rigid. She longs to be more creative and spontaneous in class, but that's impossible without departing from the teacher's guide—the ultimate cardinal sin, in her mind.

Last year, Mary attended a teacher-training workshop where she learned a number of new teaching methods. Throughout the workshop, however, one question kept nagging her: *How do I use these new methods if they aren't part of the lesson outline?*

## WHAT'S HAPPENING HERE?

Despite their differences, Joe and Mary have similar problems:

*1) They don't understand the purpose of the teacher's guide.*

Joe and Mary are expecting a curriculum writer (whom they will never meet) to create a dynamic learning environment for their particular students. That writer cannot be expected to anticipate every unusual question and unique need—or the similar types of questions and needs that Joe and Mary might have.

Mary, on the one hand, is over-dependent on the teacher's guide. For her, it takes on too much significance, and leaves her unique contributions on the sidelines. She studies the lesson plan with the level of diligence she could put into a Bible study on the lesson topic. The curriculum writer's suggestions are interpreted as absolute commands, and Mary is so afraid of violating the lesson outline that she resists the guidance and inspiration of the Holy Spirit. Mary needs to recognize that God has given her unique abilities, knowledge, and experiences that she can bring to the lesson.

Joe is just the opposite of Mary. He dismisses most of the curriculum because he lets himself get too easily frustrated by it. If the logical progression of the lesson plan is not immediately obvious to him, he rejects the entire package and does his own thing. He is a good teacher, so this method works—or at least sometimes it does. Joe is often successful, but just as often, he runs into problems. Sometimes he loses his train of thought during class because he hasn't had time to put his "homemade" lesson into a logical order.

Worse yet, as he "wings it" from his own limited knowledge, all the lessons begin to sound the same. He wants to teach with more depth, but all his preparation time is spent creating a lesson "from scratch." That doesn't leave much room in his schedule for prayer and Bible study—the things that make for a meatier presentation. Joe has to learn to work with his curriculum. When he runs into problems with the standardized lesson, he needs an alternative to "doing his own thing."

*2) They don't understand the relationship between preparation and spontaneity.*

Mary values and practices preparation, and Joe values and practices spontaneity, but they don't realize that proper preparation allows for spontaneity. If Mary prepared in a way that suited her gifts, the planning not only would take less time and trouble, but also the lesson would become her own. She could be comfortable and confident in front of her class, and an unexpected question would not faze her. If she didn't know the answer, she'd have no problem promising a response when she had some time to do a little specialized digging.

Joe needs to know how to best prepare so that he can capitalize on his natural spontaneity. He also needs to control his free-spirited style so that the lesson doesn't go off on a tangent—or into a rut. When Joe begins to "wing it," the lesson tends to jump onto one of his favorite soap boxes, and the freshness of his presentation is lost. If he prepared in a way that suited his gifts, he would appropriate the best material from the standardized curriculum. Then his spontaneous style would benefit from some direction, and the lesson would be Bible-centered and effective.

*3) They don't understand that every lesson follows a basic pattern.*

Although Joe and Mary use the teacher's guide to maintain the structure of the lesson, they don't seem to notice that each week's material follows a basic pattern. Experienced teachers learn to keep their eyes open for this recurring pattern; it is "insider's information" that helps them work with the curriculum to create a lesson that is customized to their needs. It also enables them to relax their grip on the curriculum when necessary without getting lost. If Mary understood this, she could spend less time trying to memorize details and more time absorbing the Scripture on which the lesson is based. If

Joe understood this basic pattern, he could capitalize on his spontaneity while still having order and structure to his lesson.

## TEACHING FROM THE HEART

Both Joe and Mary know their Sunday school classes are in the doldrums, but they can't seem to figure out why. Should they switch curriculum every six months, trying to find the "perfect" material? Should they run from one training seminar to another, in hopes of discovering the one "right" way to teach? What's the problem here? Is there a solution?

The problem here is not the classroom leader or the curriculum—it's the very nature of teaching. You cannot really reach students unless what you are teaching comes from your own heart. When Christ taught his disciples, everyone noticed how "he taught as one who had authority, and not as their teachers of the law" (Matt. 7:29). His response was that He spoke only what He received from His Father (John 7:16). In the same way, we need to be teachers who have been entrusted to effectively communicate God's truth to others. We need to learn the truth of what we are teaching before we can teach it to others.

Does that mean standardized curriculum is to be rejected? Not at all! Joe and Mary have missed the secret to lesson preparation: *customizing the curriculum to fit your natural teaching style and the unique needs of your students.* The best curriculum is written to be customized in this way, but many teachers have no idea how to do it. This book will show you how to use the tools of the curriculum writer to adapt a lesson so that it always meets the unique needs of your students. Before we take a look at customizing curriculum, however, there is one more teacher I'd like you to meet:

## WILLING BUT WONDERING

When Chuck was asked to teach a Sunday school class, his initial reaction was, "Who—*me?*" After being assured it wasn't just a clerical error, he agreed to pray about it—but he was still a bit puzzled.

Chuck thought about teachers he knew and wondered if he fit the mold. He didn't even know if he could define "the mold." Was he old enough, young enough, tall enough, short enough, muscular enough, skinny enough? Was his hair the right length? Did he dress like a Sunday school teacher?

After he prayed more, Chuck realized that his worries about appearance were silly. But behind all these superficial questions were a couple questions that were deeper and much more troubling: Did he know the Bible well enough to teach others? And did he have the time to prepare adequately?

*I've learned a few things about the Word,* he said to himself, *but I'm no Bible scholar. And I'm a busy guy—though I'm probably no busier than anyone else. I really don't know if I'm cut out for this.*

But Chuck did know he loved the Lord and was growing in his walk with Him. He knew he had spiritual gifts, and he wanted to use them. So he continued to pray, and he sought counsel from other mature Christians to reach his decision.

"OK, I'll teach," Chuck finally said. "What's next?"

Now he needs practical help—tools. And he needs answers for his many questions.

---

**But most of all, we want to encourage you to let go of the teacher's guide, step out onto the high wire of creativity and confidence, to really begin to teach— with all your heart.**

Whether you are a Roger, Joe, Mary, or Chuck, this book is for you. The following chapters seek to break down the stereotypes surrounding Sunday school teaching, challenging you to find your own style of teaching, and show you how to use it effectively. But most of all, we want to encourage you to relax your grip, (a little), on your teacher's guide, step out onto the high wire of creativity and confidence, and really begin to teach—with all your heart.

# Chapter One

# Where Do
# You Fit In?

WHEN WE LEFT CHUCK HE HAD JUST SAID HE WOULD TEACH, BUT NOW HE WAS HAVING SECOND THOUGHTS. His biggest concern was knowing why he had been asked to teach. Was this the Lord's will, or was he just persuaded by the Sunday school director's impassioned plea? (Some have been known to get down on their knees and beg!) Did his love for kids sway his decision, or did being asked to teach simply appeal to his pride? Was this really what God wanted him to do?

Chuck turned to the Word of God and made some interesting discoveries:

*1) Jesus gave a clear example for teachers.* Jesus spent much of His time teaching. He taught His disciples to pray (Luke 11:2-4), and He taught them how He would fulfill the prophecies about Him in the Old Testament. He told them the Holy Spirit would teach them what to say when questioned (Luke 12:12) and would teach them "all things" when He was gone (John 14:26). Jesus' teaching was also not limited to a classroom: He taught in the synagogue (Mark 6:2), in the city (Matt. 11:1), and by the seashore (Mark 4:1).

2) *Jesus expected His followers to be teachers, too.* Our Lord's last words before He ascended to heaven included the command to teach others (Matt. 28:20); teaching is obviously a ministry that is very close to God's heart. He cautioned us that how we teach and practice His commands would affect our status in the kingdom of heaven (Matt. 5:19), and James advised that not many should take up this ministry because teachers receive a stricter judgment (Jas. 3:1). These warnings show that teaching is not for everyone—but it's also not limited to the ordained, degreed professional. It is part of Christ's Great Commission to the Church.

3) *Jesus provided the power to teach.* Jesus equipped His followers for service by providing them with spiritual gifts (Rom. 12:5-6; 1 Pet. 4:10). Teaching is one of the gifts designed to perfect the Church (Rom. 12:7; 1 Cor. 12:28; Eph. 4:11). Failure to exercise those gifts weakens the ministry of the Body of Christ (1 Cor. 12:12-27).

## IS TEACHING MY GIFT?

Seeing Jesus' example as a teacher, His command to teach, and His equipping through spiritual gifts, Chuck was still unsure of just where he fit in. In the interest of seeking godly counsel, he decided to talk with his Sunday school director, Bob.

"Bob, I have a question for you," Chuck said as they sat down over runny eggs and dry toast at the local diner. "How can I be sure I have the gift of teaching?"

Bob's eyes started to twinkle. "So you're having second thoughts about taking that class?" He grinned as Chuck nodded and shared the results of his Bible study on teaching.

"The fact that your first instinct was to look into the Word is a positive indicator to me," Bob noted. "Tell me, can you think of anything that proves that you don't have the gift of teaching?"

"Well, I've never taught before."

"And, so . . . ?"

"Bob, I've been a Christian for several years. Wouldn't a spiritual gift of teaching show up by now?"

Bob laughed. "You were expecting it to arrive by special delivery?"

Chuck grinned sheepishly and mumbled, "Well, but . . ."

"Chuck, you may not be teaching a Sunday school class right now—not yet, at least—but I know you'd make a great teacher. When we were in that Bible study together last year, you asked some really great questions that made us think. I know I learned a lot from you."

Chuck's eyebrows rose, and he opened his mouth to speak, but Bob was just warming up.

"The church has several teaching positions to fill every quarter, Chuck. A few of our teachers can serve year after year, but most of them need a break after a few quarters. That means the church needs a lot of people involved in teaching! But don't you think that at least some of them are less than 100% confident of their ability to do the job when they first begin?"

Chuck shrugged.

---

**"I think God is more concerned about people being available than people being doubt-free because He's the One who provides the grace to do the work, anyway."**

---

"I'll tell you what I think," Bob continued. "I think God is more concerned about people being available than people being doubt-free because He's the one who provides the grace to do the work, anyway. But if you're still concerned about whether you have the gift of teaching, let me give you a few questions to ponder."

While Chuck munched thoughtfully on an English muffin, Bob wrote down the following questions on a napkin:

- Am I diligent in the study of God's Word?
- Do I enjoy researching biblical truths?
- Am I anxious to share my discoveries with others?
- Do I solve problems by going to Scripture?
- Am I concerned that God's truth is always presented?
- Am I discerning about where I obtain information?
- Do I want to see others grow in their Christian faith?
- Do I have an interest in students from a particular age group and how they learn?

As Chuck prayerfully considered these questions, he became convinced that he should accept the teaching position. First, however, he wanted to get an idea of what to expect. So he talked to two of the teachers introduced previously, Joe and Mary, and observed their Sunday school classes.

Unfortunately, his observations raised more doubts in his mind. He couldn't identify with either teacher's approach. He felt that Joe was too "unprepared" and Mary too "cut and dried," and it appeared that they both lacked freedom to be themselves and take the class in a particular direction. He wondered if he had to settle for one approach or the other.

Chuck decided that he would learn by doing, and he began to pray that God would equip him to become the teacher He wanted him to be. But he also realized he needed help and support from other teachers.

When he talked to Joe and Mary, he was surprised to find that they had doubts and questions about their teaching as well. The three agreed to meet for prayer and discussion about their teaching ministry.

---

**You can be an effective teacher, even if you don't "fit the mold."**

---

Chuck, Mary, and Joe were about to learn something that would change their teaching forever: You can be an effective teacher, even if you don't "fit the mold." The secret is in learning to customize your curriculum—to tailor it to yourself and the unique needs of your students. Instead of trying to fit someone else's mold, make your own.

We all have unique talents and abilities that we bring to our teaching. In addition, each of us is more comfortable with certain activities and types of presentations. You need to capitalize on your special abilities as you approach each teaching opportunity. And don't be shy about continuing to use teaching methods that are tried-and-true for you—as long as you're willing to move out of your "comfort zone" once in a while.

Are you and your students more comfortable with a lecture-type approach? Or do you and they like to get involved in lively discussions and hands-on activities? You may find that the way you learn most effectively is the teaching style you lean toward using. But be sure to always keep the learning styles of your students in mind.

Consider the different classrooms in which you have participated as a student. Which ones did you enjoy the most? What was it about those classes and teachers that made them so enjoyable and stimulating to you? Did you most enjoy what the teacher had to say? The class discussion? The opportunity to look at a picture or map? Or was it perhaps the chance to make something with your hands?

As you begin to understand what kind of learner you are, it can help you identify which teaching style is most comfortable for you. This process should also start you thinking about the types of students in your classroom.

The crucial question is, just how do your students learn best? Each learner in your classroom will give a different answer to that question. You need to reach them in the style that best suits their learning needs.

That is why it is best to offer several kinds of approaches and activities during one class period. This is especially important with children who lack the motivation and attention span necessary to learn outside their natural learning style. (In a nutshell, the four types of learners include: 1. Imaginative; 2. Analytical; 3. Common Sense; and 4. Dynamic or Visionary. You'll read more about these learning styles in Chapter 3.) Unless you touch upon all four learning styles during the lesson, you cannot be sure that you are reaching each of them. (A helpful resource on these four types of learning styles is a book by Marlene LeFever called *Learning Styles: Reaching Everyone God Gave You to Teach*—it's available online at www.cookministries.com or you can pick it up at your local Christian bookstore.)

The problem, of course, with providing a variety of activities is that some of them may not be as comfortable for you to teach. That's part of being a teacher in the body of Christ—you have to learn to stretch yourself. As you plan and implement these new approaches and methods, you may find that you enjoy them more than you thought you would.

What unique aspects of your life and personality can you apply to your teaching? How exactly can you adapt your curriculum on a week-by-week, lesson-by-lesson basis to fit your teaching style and the learning styles of your students? To answer these questions we need to consider how curriculum is produced in the first place.

## DOES ONE SIZE FIT ALL?

Standardized curriculum is designed to cover all the bases. The typical lesson may include:

- A community-building, "Why are we studying this?" activity
- A Bible-content section
- A variety of activities related to the Bible story
- A verse to memorize
- A "Relate-it-to-life" section

Why are lessons set up like this? Lessons that are set up like this follow the natural learning cycle of capturing the students' attention, learning the facts, practicing what we learned, and making a plan to implement the Bible truths learned throughout the week.

But, by necessity, these publishers are "shooting for the middle"—they have a general idea of what teachers will need during the lesson, but they clearly expect every teacher to take the material and customize it for their particular students. A common complaint of many teachers is that there is often too much material available. Some publishers do this on purpose because it's "better to have it and not need it, than to need it, and not have it." But if the lesson is followed as if it were merely a screenplay for the class, the teacher would never get through all the material.

Other publishers have gone to the opposite extreme and have essentially reduced their curriculum to a single, high-energy activity for the entire lesson. The perceptive teacher can immediately see the flaws in this type of approach. How much content is actually taught? What if the teacher is not a "high-energy" person? Wouldn't this method get "old" after a while? And though it may work well with some age groups, (perhaps with kids loaded with lots of sugar) it probably would border on the ridiculous with others—like the "golden-agers" class, for example!

## THE TEACHER IS THE KEY

In all this, one main ingredient can easily be lost: the teacher. If God has gifted the teacher, then the effectiveness of the lesson must depend on the gifted person (who in turn is focused on the needs of the students) and not the mere script of a curriculum. The curriculum is not the problem, but it's not the solution, either. Creativity, spontaneity, and "lesson ownership" have to come from you, the teacher. Often this process consists of picturing the lesson elements in your mind and seeing them fit into a pattern that is simpler and more familiar for you.

Every lesson needs to follow a regular, logical pattern that you can keep in your head while teaching. Each lesson has to be formed into a road map, to "get you from point A to point B."

If the lesson follows the same pattern each week, does this mean the class becomes dull and repetitive? Not at all. The regular pattern must be simple but easily adaptable, so you can keep your lessons fresh by using a variety of teaching methods—while keeping the same simple steps in mind.

The next chapter explains this logical pattern and shows how to adapt a standardized lesson to your own style.

**THINKING IT OVER:**

1) What things in your life communicate that you may have the gift of teaching?

2) Not all of us have the gift of evangelism, but we are all called to be a witness for Christ. How might that relate to the gift of teaching?

3) Roger's story shows how one man used his experience and expertise to enhance his teaching. What unique experiences and expertise do you have that you could bring to the Sunday school classroom?

**MAKING IT WORK:**

Interview a number of Sunday school teachers about their reasons for teaching. Ask them to share how God has used their unique experiences, skills, and abilities in their teaching.

# <u>Notes</u>

# Chapter Two

# A Map of
# the Territory

I USUALLY START BY TEARING MY HAIR OUT," JOE SAID WITH A SMIRK. He was responding to Chuck's question about how he prepared for his Sunday school class.

"Why? What's so frustrating?" Chuck asked.

"Well, sometimes the material brings up stuff that I've never heard of—but I have a sneaking suspicion that I should know what it's talking about. Take last week's lesson, for instance. After the Bible story, the teacher's guide instructs you to take the children over to the activity center. What's an 'activity center'?"

"Oh, I can explain that," Mary said confidently. "In the beginning of the teacher's guide, it suggests you divide your classroom into four sections. The activity center is the area they designate for craft projects and such."

"So that's how you set up your classroom?" Chuck asked.

"Well, no," she replied, looking like a kid caught with her hand in the cookie jar. "You see, my classroom is too small for that. We do everything on one table in the middle of the room."

"That must make it pretty hard to do a craft," Chuck observed.

"Everything has to be cleaned up and put away before you can go on to the next part of the lesson."

"Yes, exactly!" Mary agreed, obviously relieved that someone understood. "And then I have trouble finishing the lesson on time. I'm afraid to cut something out for the sake of time because I don't always see how the different pieces of the lesson plan fit together. But what else can I do?"

"When I encounter a problem like that," Joe said, "I just dump the whole lesson and come up with something on my own."

Mary stared at Joe in shocked silence as Chuck said, "Seems a little extreme, Joe. Maybe there's a middle road between following the teacher's guide word-for-word and replacing the lesson completely."

Chuck was beginning to understand the concept of customizing curriculum and "lesson ownership."

\* \* \* \* \*

## THE CURRICULUM "MAP"

---

**What exactly is curriculum, anyway? Dr. Joe D. Marlow concludes that it is best understood using the metaphor of a map—a tool to help you find your direction and get from one place to another.**

---

What exactly is curriculum, anyway? Dr. Joe D. Marlow concludes that it is best understood using the metaphor of a map—a tool to help you find your direction and get from one place to another.[1]

The map metaphor is a brilliant description of the kind of help a teacher needs, and the typical standardized Sunday school curriculum appears to be based on that metaphor. Written in a complete, step-by-step format, the lessons in most published teacher's guides are built on a learning objective (often called the "aim" or "focus" of the lesson), which is a statement of what the student is expected to learn.

You have a single goal—the lesson aim—and a step-by-step program to reach it. If only it were that simple!

## UNFOCUSED AIMS

The first monkey wrench thrown into the gears of the lesson may come directly from the hand of the curriculum writer. The teacher looks for a lesson focus or aim that provides a clear goal to shoot for and sometimes finds one that is hard to measure. What is the focus/aim of the lesson? How can you tell if it works?

Even if a lesson has a clear aim, many teachers are looking for Dr. Marlow's metaphor—a map of the territory more than a description of the final destination. In other words, having a "goal" for the lesson is not enough; most teachers expect the lesson to consist of a series of steps toward that goal. If a curriculum is well-done, it will provide these things for you.

A fuzzy example of a focus/aim written for an adult may say something like, "The student will appreciate the depth of Christ's sacrifice." A poor example of a focus/aim written for elementary-age material may say something like, "The children will see God as a big helper." These statements make it difficult to measure and fail to provide clear direction for the lesson. Without a clearly-defined focus, the lesson is more difficult to teach.

Let's take the adult lesson aim mentioned previously: "The student will appreciate the depth of Christ's sacrifice." What does the writer mean by "depth"? Perhaps all the aspects of Christ's sacrifice should be listed. Of course, you need some way to introduce the topic. Perhaps a reading of the Gospel accounts of the crucifixion would be a good way to start.

The same principle is true of a lesson focus written for children. What does the writer mean by "seeing God as a big helper"? First of all, the children should understand the ways we can approach God to ask for His help. The best way to do this is through an example, since children are rarely able to think in abstract terms about such a subject. It would be helpful for them to think about how they approach their parents or a teacher when they ask for help. In other words, bring it down to their level. Then we could move on to the Bible lesson where an example from Scripture helps the children understand that people have always asked God for help. Because of different learning styles, some students may still not grasp the point. Therefore, some children may need to have an activity to reinforce the subject or a craft where they make something that helps them grasp and understand the concept. Again, a curriculum that is well-done will provide these types of helps for you—but you are the one who breathes life into them for your particular students.

The adult students in our example need to be confronted with the question, "How does Christ's sacrifice apply to me?" before they can really appreciate the depth. You want your students to "own" the lesson truth so they will apply it whenever appropriate. Obviously, this can be done in different ways. After you, the teacher, have presented the material, the student must not only be told how it can apply to his or her life, but must also internalize it or make a plan to apply the truth. In the case of children, the plan might include listing ways they can ask for God's help with a particular problem or difficult situation in their lives. They might need to place that list on their closet door or the refrigerator to help them remember.

Do you see how the lesson focus or aim, when analyzed, becomes a *process?* What could be nothing more than a vague, ambitious goal has now become a fairly clear set of steps. A perceptive teacher will be consciously looking for steps such as these. Let's review them in terms of the adult lesson:

1) Introduce topic with Gospel accounts of crucifixion.

2) List the aspects of Christ's sacrifice.

3) Show how it applies to the student's life.

4) Challenge them to use the truth outside the classroom.

If the teacher can perform these steps, the chances are good that many of the students will accomplish the lesson aim and learn to "appreciate the depth of Christ's sacrifice" or "think about ways to ask for God's help." Of course, how to practice these steps is still unclear. But that's what the rest of the lesson plan is all about, isn't it? That's where you can partner with the curriculum writer to bring life and excitement to your Sunday school classroom.

## PITY THE POOR CURRICULUM WRITER

Curriculum writing is a tough job. As was noted in the previous chapter, the material has to be written to cover all the bases, to meet the needs of every student. It includes such things as ongoing projects, high-activity exercises, and "community-building" activities. It can be very difficult to include all these elements and still stick to the lesson aim. Other problems frequently encountered by the curriculum writers as they try to anticipate the teachers' needs include: a variety of time restraints, limited facilities, available personnel, past failures, class sizes, church budgets, and anticipating the unexpected.

## CUSTOMIZING YOUR CURRICULUM

To solve these kinds of problems, a teacher must learn to customize the curriculum so that he or she "owns" the lesson by the time the class begins. The curriculum writer realizes you may encounter some or all of the problems listed above. The writer also realizes that you may not be able to do all the elements of the lesson. You are expected and encouraged to pick and choose the ones that fit best with your situation.

Let's consider how to customize the curriculum based on some typical problems that are frequently encountered by teachers.

*Time restraints . . . Too much curriculum for the time you have.* The curriculum writer has typically provided enough material to cover class periods as long as 60 minutes. Yet some teachers have only 40 minutes. What do you do? You need to choose the activities that will best cover the lesson while still taking into account the limited amount of time. Be sure to introduce the lesson in personal and understandable ways for your students. Present the Scripture lesson, and give the students a chance to practice or understand the lesson in a "hands-to-heart manner." Finally, allow enough time to be sure your students have grasped the lesson in a way that they can apply it to their own lives during the coming week.

*Limited Facilities . . . Little or no room for games and exercises.* Some churches may lack the space for certain activities. Some games and exercises may assume that you have a large classroom, or the freedom to be "loud," or that you have special materials or equipment. Does that mean you can never do them? Look for alternatives. Is the weather nice? Can you take your class outside for a 10-minute activity where the space and noise are no longer a problem? Is there another activity included in the material that you can choose instead? Can you adapt the activity to a smaller space?

*Personnel . . . No one to help.* Some lesson plans may include an activity that requires an adult assistant or a "special guest"—but some teachers don't have anyone to help them. If you are working with children, consider asking a teenager to be your assistant for the day or for part of the class, or ask a parent to assist you. If you are working with adults, you can ask one of your students to be your assistant.

*Past Failures* . . . *Afraid to try again.* A teacher should be willing to try new methods, and even try them repeatedly if they are not successful the first time, but some teachers know that certain projects and exercises are too unpopular, difficult, or disruptive for their situation. If you have found a particular activity or exercise troublesome, consider redesigning the activity to make it work for your situation. Or, if you have found an activity that works especially well, consider revising it to use in a new situation. Failures can be positive. They can help you learn how to make the situation better in the future.

*Class Size* . . . *"Groups of three? I only have four in the class!"* If you have a small class of students, you can work as one group. You can still do the activity, but think about how it will work for just one group. If the activity requires three students, it can probably just as easily be done with two or four. Also consider yourself a participant in a group if necessary.

*Church Budgets* . . . *"My church could barely afford the curriculum — where am I going to get 'chenille wires'?"* Many churches do not have a fully-stocked Sunday school supply cabinet, filled with construction paper, craft sticks, glue, scissors, etc. If a craft or activity calls for a particular item that your church does not have, look for readily-available or inexpensive items. Many teachers buy what they need out of their own pockets. Some consider this part of their giving to the church, but for others this can be quite burdensome. Consider asking the parents of your students (if you're teaching children) to contribute the needed supplies. You might be surprised at their willingness to help you out.

*The Unexpected* . . . *Anything can happen.* A last-minute change of personnel or facilities, an unplanned delay that eats up valuable class time, a sudden increase or decrease in attendance—any of these can make an inflexible lesson plan impossible to implement. Keep in mind that anytime you are teaching, the unexpected question or situation can come up. That's part of the excitement of teaching for God! Flexibility is the key to making it work. In preparing your lesson, it doesn't hurt to have alternate plans in case you run short of time or a few extra students show up.

Typically, teachers find that time restraints, resource limitations, and other problems may make it necessary to alter the lesson. What you need now is an outline, a framework, or to use Marlow's metaphor, a map. Your curriculum is most likely based on an outline or map planned by the curriculum writer. Generally speaking, this takes the form of a three-point outline.

## THE THREE-POINT OUTLINE

Fortunately, there is a tried-and-true three-point lesson outline, one which has its roots in antiquity. *Every lesson has a beginning, a middle, and an end.* Let's look again at the three points we pulled out of the lesson aim:

1) Introduce topic with Gospel accounts of crucifixion.

2) List the aspects of Christ's sacrifice.

3) Show how it applies to the student's life.

Notice how "beginning, middle, end" fits these three steps. The first is an *introduction* to the lesson; the second is the *body* of the material being presented; and the third is the *conclusion*.

Introduction: Why are we talking about this?

Body: What is it and what does it all mean?

Conclusion: What does it mean for me?

The three-point lesson is simple and natural, but also flexible enough to be molded into different versions. They come in many colors—you're sure to find one that is right for you!

For example, one version of the three-point method is used for inductive Bible study. I remember it with the acronym *OIL*—Observation, Interpretation, and Life application.

- Observation: What does the Scripture passage *say?*
- Interpretation: What does the passage *mean?*
- Life application: What does it mean *for me?*

You can use the three-point method for a topical study as well in three different "views":

- Preview: An initial "view" of the topic,
- Overview: A comprehensive "view,"
- Review: A parting "view."

A controversial issue-oriented lesson might be seen in this format:

- Question: What is the issue?
- Discussion: What are the points under dispute?
- Resolution: How does Scripture settle the conflict?

And there are many other possible ways to view the three-point format. Use your imagination.

Some teacher guides split their lessons into four steps, but your three-point outline still applies. In four-step lessons, combine Steps 2 and 3 to make up the "body" step of the Introduction, Body, and Conclusion outline. For example, a four-step lesson might ask these educational questions

- Why is this important? [Introduction]
- What do I need to know? [Body - First Part]
- How can we make it work? [Body - Second Part]
- What can it become outside the classroom? [Conclusion - making a plan to apply the Bible truth in real life.]

The logical progression of this three-point outline makes it easy to implement. As long as you keep a basic outline in your head, you never have to worry about getting "lost" in the middle of the lesson. A student can ask a question, a mishap can occur or your notes may get out of order, and you will still be in control.

## DON'T FORGET THE AIM!

---

**Think of the lesson aim as an arrow with three steps as the targets. The goal is to shoot the arrow through the center of all the targets consecutively.**

---

What about the lesson aim? This is the outline's unifying element. The aim should be woven through the entire lesson. Think of the lesson aim as an arrow with three steps as the targets. The goal is to shoot the arrow through the center of all the targets consecutively.

The focus/aim can help you stay on track as you customize the lesson. If time restraints, resource limitations, and other problems make it necessary to weed out elements of the lesson, what elements do you keep and what do you throw away? Your focus/aim will help you determine relevance for each element. Does each lesson element deal directly with the topic at hand? Does it take the class toward the ultimate goal of the lesson? If not, cut it out.

The lesson aim, by the way, should be customized as well. C. Doug Bryan points out that the goal of a lesson should "emerge from two basic sources—needs of the learner and the material under investigation."[2] With that in mind, teachers should adapt the lesson aim to the unique needs of their classes. Sharpening the focus of the aim will be discussed in the next chapter.

## THE BENEFITS OF THE THREE-POINT OUTLINE

The three-point outline is very flexible and can be implemented in almost any teaching situation. Even if the lesson plan in your teacher's guide happens to fit your circumstances well, and you feel you can teach it "as-is," with little or no modifications, there are still a number of good reasons for using one of the outlines.

*1) They are the natural way to learn.* Your students grow to expect the material to be introduced, presented, and applied to daily life, all focusing on a central truth. It may be subconscious, but it is still noticeable in the way your class responds. A familiar pattern will keep students from getting lost or confused.

*2) They are also the natural way to teach.* The simple, logical progression of a three-point outline helps you keep the plan in your head and avoid those long, awkward pauses as you search your notes to find your place. When you aren't worried about getting lost, you can relax and be more spontaneous in your teaching.

*3) They accommodate various learning styles.* Marlene LeFever says that students respond to a lesson with at least one of four different questions:

- Why do I need to know this?
- What do I need to know?
- How does this work?
- What can this become?

By the way, these questions represent what's most important to the four different types of learners.[3]

Both the three-point outline and the lesson aim can answer all of these questions and reach every type of learner in your class. How you can do this will be covered in the next chapter.

4) *The outline frees your mind to focus on student feedback.* When you can relax your grip on the teacher's guide, you can catch the subtle cues that help you know if your students are learning. My son had a chance to talk to folk singer Livingston Taylor after a concert and asked what advice he had for a young musician.

"Watch your audience," Taylor answered. "When they're smiling and attentive, keep doing what you're doing. If they're not smiling, cut it out!" That's good advice for a teacher!

5) *Finally, the three-point outline makes your teaching goal-oriented.* Every part of the lesson is directed toward driving home the lesson aim. As was said before, think of the aim as an arrow and the three steps as the targets.

How do you adapt curriculum to these formats? Does every lesson need to be adapted? That is what we'll discuss in the next chapter.

**THINKING IT OVER:**

1) What problems have you encountered in trying to faithfully follow the teacher's guide?

2) Does the three-point outline seem "natural" to you?

3) In what situations have you used or seen others use a three-point outline? How did they work?

**MAKING IT WORK:**

Using a lesson from a standardized curriculum, try reworking it into a three-point outline. Concentrate on making the outline conform to the lesson focus/aim. Do not be concerned about making the outline too detailed. Then show the outline to another teacher to get feedback.

# Notes

# Chapter Three

# Customizing the Lesson

THE THREE TEACHERS WERE MEETING IN MARY'S KITCHEN. Of course, every utensil, dish, and spice was exactly in its proper place—where it belonged.

"I'm feeling a bit more comfortable with not including everything suggested in the lesson plan," she began shyly. "But it isn't easy; a lot of times the different elements are interconnected. Last week the lesson plan called for a rather involved game, and I couldn't find the time or materials, so I dropped it. What I hadn't noticed was that other parts of the lesson referred to the game! Finally, I had to tell the kids about the game and promise that we'd play it sometime. How do I get myself into these things?"

Chuck and Joe laughed a little, but they both sympathized.

"Don't feel bad, Mary; it's happened to me before, too," Joe said. "The part of the lesson that you think is optional turns out to be essential. You pull out one brick, and the whole wall seems to tumble down!"

"I guess," Chuck replied, "the only solution is to rebuild the wall—brick by brick."

\* \* \* \* \*

Whenever you start removing elements from your curriculum, you can find yourself left with a dismembered lesson plan. That's where the map of your lesson comes in. How do we reconstruct the lesson using the three-point outline?

## SHARPENING THE AIM

The first step is to analyze the focus of the lesson and determine if it needs to be more sharply focused. If it's well-written, leave it alone. The focus should state what the student will be able to do with the content of the lesson, rather than about the content itself. Gary Dean refers to this as LWBAT—"the Learner Will Be Able To . . ."[1] Is the aim clearly stated? Is it measurable? Is it specific enough to build the three-point outline upon it, but open-ended enough for those dreamers and visionaries in your class to add new ideas and possibilities to it?

You could write a lesson as specific as, "The student will be able to name three aspects of forgiveness." An effective lesson plan for such an aim would be easy; it could be as simplistic as an hour-long training session in rote memorization of the "three aspects." But would any real learning take place?

If you change such an aim to make it less "mind" and more "heart," you may come up with something such as, "The student will be able to appreciate the various aspects of forgiveness." But how is appreciation measurable? It ends up being as vague as the aims mentioned in the previous chapter.

It should be apparent by now that lesson aims are hard to write. The aim given in your teacher's guide may not be as focused as you might like it to be, but try to see how you can work with it. If the aim is clear enough to give you an idea of where the lesson is headed, you should be able to use it with just a little fine-tuning. Some lessons will have "mini-aims" at the beginning of each section that are more behavior-oriented than the over-arching lesson focus—if these are present, use them to help shape your "three-point mind-outline."

Let's take the aim stated previously: "The student will be able to appreciate the various aspects of forgiveness." It is clear that the topic is forgiveness and that the content of the lesson will include the different aspects of forgiveness. The problem is in the verb "appreciate" which is an inward feeling and hard to measure. The verb in the aim has to be an outward action.

This outward action must be one that is open-ended and applies to the student's Christian walk. The aim, "The student will be able to name three aspects of forgiveness," doesn't work because there aren't many creative ways to "name" something. Besides that, naming aspects of forgiveness will not lead to a change in the student's life. The lesson aim has to involve creative application and personal involvement.

A better lesson aim might be, "The student will be able to incorporate forgiveness into his or her relationships." It gives a clear idea of the lesson content, it is a measurable action, it allows for creative possibilities, and it calls for personal change.

What is needed here is a marriage of mind and heart, something that occurs best in a real-life situation. Another way to express the aim might be, "The student will be able to apply three aspects of forgiveness in a real life situation." In this aim, we are identifying a measurable, outward action that reflects an inward heart attitude.

## TEST THE BIBLICAL FOUNDATION

The next step is to analyze the Scriptures cited in the lesson and how each is used. Be like the Bereans and "search the Scriptures" (Acts 17:11) to make sure that your curriculum is clearly presenting biblical truth. If the Apostle Paul was held accountable in this way, certainly your curriculum deserves the same scrutiny. Do the verses in the teacher's guide relate to the aim of the lesson? If not, find other verses, or alter the lesson aim. Scripture takes precedence over the lesson aim. If you can't find a biblical foundation for the aim, change it!

Do not allow the lesson aim to color your interpretation of the Bible. An article in *Christian Education Journal* tells the story of a father whose preschooler had learned about Cain and Abel in Sunday school. Wondering how the teacher had handled such a complex story of sacrifice, murder, and judgment, the father asked, "What did you find out about Cain and Abel?"

"God made their bodies," came the nonchalant reply.

"What did Cain and Abel do?" the father asked.

"They didn't do anything."

As it turned out, the child had not been forgetful or inattentive. In fact, he quoted the point of the lesson almost verbatim: "God made our bodies." The authors of the article commented, "If the Bible is used only as a jump-off point for one's own education objectives, the Bible's authority is being bypassed. . . . Too much of today's curriculum teaches only with human authority rather than with the authority of God."[2]

In this case, the curriculum was working with a thoroughly biblical aim—"God made our bodies" is certainly taught in Scripture—but just NOT in the story of Cain and Abel. The lesson aim, while totally appropriate for preschoolers, was based on an inappropriate passage of Scripture. Lesson aims need to be (1) age-appropriate and (2) Bible-passage appropriate. If they're not one or the other, either change the aim or switch the Bible story so that both criteria are met. For this reason, you should avoid Sunday school curriculum that covers the same Bible passage at all age levels preschool through adult.

Principles for confirming and strengthening the biblical

foundation of your lesson will be discussed in Chapter Four.

## CHOOSING TEACHING METHODS

Teaching methods are the vehicle in which you carry the lesson to the students. Whether it is lecture, discussion, a skit, or a craft, teaching methods build on the lesson's focus/aim. If the methods in the teacher's guide do not suit your situation (if you lack the materials for a craft, for example), replace them; there are plenty to choose from. You can also prepare alternate methods to plan for the unexpected (last-minute changes in facilities, class size, etc.), as was mentioned in Chapter Two.

Usually, at least one different teaching method should be used for each of the three or four parts of your lesson outline. An overview of various methods, along with their strengths and weaknesses, is presented in Chapter Five and Appendix B.

## PRESENTATION AND EVALUATION

Each section in the three-point outline has three sections as well:

1) An opening statement that leads the class into the teaching method,

2) The teaching method,

3) A closing statement that wraps up the section and moves the lesson to the next stage.

The opening and closing statements are often called transitions. These are critical parts of the lesson because they prevent the "awkward pauses" that every teacher dreads. Transitions keep the students attentive and help the teacher cope with the fear of being "on stage." A good transition can be a question, a provocative statement, a short poem or jingle, or even just a word or two of instruction. The effective use of transitions is covered in Chapter Six.

The topics covered so far are techniques of lesson preparation; there are also techniques of lesson presentation—useful tips for the classroom situation. Chapter Seven explains how to tie it all together during the class period while Chapter Eight will explain how to evaluate the effectiveness of your presentation, both during and after the class.

---

**The lesson aim flows through the entire lesson, supported by its scriptural foundation.**

---

The three points of the mental outline of your lesson are tied together by the transitional material of openings and closings. Between each opening and closing is the teaching method for that section of the lesson. The lesson aim flows through the entire lesson, supported by its scriptural foundation.

## FINDING THE TIME

All well and good, you may say, but who has the time to do this much preparation? In reality, the three-point outline is really a time-saver. Any attempt to prepare for class with a standardized lesson plan can be very time-consuming. It can take hours to become familiar enough with someone else's plan to be able to present it smoothly. But customizing your lesson can take as little as 15 to 30 minutes a day— or less than two hours if you choose to do it in one sitting. Later chapters explain how to do preparation simply and efficiently.

## PREPARATION AND LEARNING STYLES

While preparing a lesson according to the three-point outline, it is important to choose the lesson aim and teaching methods with a view to the four basic learning styles identified by Marlene LeFever:[3]

The **introduction** (first point of your three-point outline) relates to the imaginative learner who looks for the purpose of the lesson: "Why do I have to know this?" Because people learn by moving from the familiar to the unfamiliar, step one concentrates on relating the new material to existing knowledge. This part of the lesson establishes a foundation and gets everyone in the class "on the same page." It draws on the students' own interests and experiences to lead them into the Bible topic.

The **body** (second point of your three-point outline) of the lesson relates to the analytic learner who thrives on content: "What do I need to know?" Bible content is especially important here, and the analytic learner will often help the rest of the class pull out the principles inherent in the Scripture being studied. This is step two in a four-step plan.

Following up on the Bible content, the common-sense learner, asks, "How does this work?" (This is also included in the **body**, or content portion, of the three-point outline.) A real-life example makes it "click" for them. Coming up with ways to practice and apply both existing knowledge and new information to real life is the common-sense learner's forte. "Therefore every scribe instructed concerning the kingdom of heaven is like a householder who brings out of his treasure things new and old" (Matt. 13:52, NKJV).

Since in the three-point format, the body of the lesson incorporates both the analytic learner's need for content ("What do I need to know?") and the common-sense learner's need to see it in practice ("How does this work?"), it is usually the longest part of the lesson. In fact, this is why some curriculum is divided into four steps, one for each type of learning style.

The **conclusion** (third point of your three-point outline) of the lesson incorporates the lesson aim (which is threaded throughout the lesson) and appeals to the dynamic or visionary learner, the one who asks, "What can this become?" These students enjoy finding ways to take what they have learned on Sunday and use it in their lives throughout the week. The teacher needs to be an encourager during this concluding step—a step which, for the dynamic learner, continues on long after the classroom learning is over. This last step is necessary in either a three- or four-step lesson to help the student apply the lesson.

In order to keep the attention of the dynamic learner, as well as following the principle of moving from the known to the unknown, it is often helpful to avoid directly stating the lesson aim at the beginning. Instead, the lesson aim should be hinted at throughout the lesson, becoming the "rabbit out of the hat" at the end. Everything builds to the inevitable conclusion: "And the moral of the story is . . ." Jesus ended some of his parables and teachings this way, using a "therefore" statement: "Therefore be on the watch . . ." for example.

## JESUS AND LEARNING STYLES

You can see how the Master Teacher incorporated learning in Luke 10. After reviewing that God commands us to love our neighbor as ourselves, the expert in the law provides a perfect introduction by asking, "And who is my neighbor?" (10:29). He was obviously an imaginative learner!

Jesus started into the body of His lesson by telling the parable of the Good Samaritan, meeting the content need of the analytic learners in the crowd. Then He rounded out the body of the lesson with a practical question for the common-sense learner: "Which of these three do you think was a neighbor to the man who fell into the hands of robbers?"

(10:36). When the expert in the law gave the correct answer—"The one who had mercy on him"—Jesus delivered a conclusion designed to hit a dynamic learner right between the eyes: "Go and do likewise" (10:37).

## THE IMPORTANCE OF LEARNING STYLES

We tend to teach from the approach in which we learn best. In other words, the imaginative learner, for example, tends to teach with emphasis on the foundation and purpose of the lesson. Without the three-point outline, he or she may never get to the content and application of the lesson! On the other hand, a common-sense learner is very application-oriented. Such a teacher may rush to put the material into practice even though the students have not yet absorbed the content or understood the whole point of the lesson!

---

**As a teacher, you will find that lesson outline causes you to stretch your skills, so that even though you are naturally oriented toward one of the four learning styles, you will be able to include activities that will address all the styles of learners on a regular basis.**

---

The three-point outline keeps the teacher's natural tendencies in check, bringing balance and completeness to the lesson. As a teacher, you will find that the lesson outline causes you to stretch your skills, so that even though you are naturally oriented toward one of the four learning styles, you will be able to include activities that will address all the styles of learners on a regular basis.

The remaining chapters of the book will cover the various elements of the lesson in more detail, starting with the scriptural foundation.

**THINKING IT OVER:**

1) What makes a lesson aim focused and dynamic?

2) How would you focus this aim: "The student will be able to understand the meaning of grace?"

3) How does your learning style affect your teaching? What changes do you need to make in order to address the needs of all the learners in your classroom?

**MAKING IT WORK:**

Look over the lesson you outlined in Chapter Two. If the aim appears to be unfocused, try reworking it using LWBAT.

# <u>Notes</u>

# Chapter Four

# Rightly Dividing
# the Word

W HEN JOE, CHUCK, AND MARY HAD THEIR NEXT MEETING, JOE BROUGHT HIS TEACHER'S GUIDE WITH HIM. "Let me show you what I'm up against each week," Joe began. "This week's lesson, for example, is supposed to be about caring for others. But the main part of the lesson centers on the story of Jesus healing a crippled man. What does that have to do with our caring for others?"

"I guess the point of the lesson would be that Jesus showed concern for the crippled man, and so should we," Chuck answered.

"But that's the problem," Joe replied. "The lesson doesn't give practical ways we can show concern for others—or at least I'm not seeing it. I think it could give the students the impression that, unless you can heal a disabled person, there's no way to help them."

"I see what you mean," Mary said, as she reviewed the lesson. "The aim and the Scripture don't seem to fit together well, do they? You're pretty sharp, Joe. I never would have noticed that—at least not until after I finished teaching the lesson!"

"So, Joe, are you going to dump the lesson and write your own?" Chuck asked with a little smile.

"Wait a minute!" Mary cried before Joe could answer. "I see what the problem is—we haven't really seen the point of the Bible story. It isn't that Jesus had compassion on the crippled man, but that the crippled man's friends brought him to Jesus!"

Joe flipped to the passage and read it out loud, a grin slowly creeping across his face. "Wow, you're right, Mary. These guys couldn't get through the crowd, but that didn't stop them. They dug a hole in the roof and lowered their friend down. They didn't let any obstacle stop them from helping their friend. Now that's a lesson I can teach!"

---

**A key to making a lesson your own is to get a good grasp of its biblical foundation.**

---

A key to making a lesson your own is to get a good grasp of its biblical foundation. Analyzing how Scripture is used in a lesson is a fairly straightforward process. It consists of studying in depth the passage(s) used in the lesson and then comparing your conclusions with the lesson's aim and major points.

When you have collected the text(s) from the lesson, begin with prayer. Ask the Holy Spirit to help you lay aside all preconceived notions (including the lesson aim, for that matter) and to help you understand what you read. Try to forget for a moment that you are teaching, and ask to be a student at the Lord's feet.

## IMMERSE YOURSELF IN THE TEXT

Read through the passage(s) at least three times in one sitting. Spend some time mulling over the words; take notes as well. See how another translation of the Scriptures phrases the passage(s). Seek to enjoy God's Word. Catch the passion of Paul Little who said, "Bible study is like eating peanuts. The more you eat, the more you want to eat."[1]

As you read, ask yourself:

- What is the main idea of the passage (in a single sentence)?
- If it is a narrative passage, who are the main characters?
- If it is an expository passage, what is the line of argument?

Write down your answers. Don't be discouraged if the answers seem incomplete or unclear; they will be fleshed out as you study more. Also write down a list of the major nouns in the passage, to clarify what is being discussed. List the verbs in the passage to clarify the action taking place. Then list the modifiers (adjectives and adverbs) to make the description in the passage stand out. Do you notice repeated phrases? They are not there by accident; list those as well. Listing the nouns, verbs, modifiers, and repeated phrases can help you catch the vision and intent of the biblical writer.

Another way to find meaning through the words is to look for poetic devices in the passage. The biblical writers used similes, metaphors, and various other techniques. Here are just a few:

- Apostrophe is a direct address to something or someone who is absent or cannot respond, as in "Where, O death, is your sting?" (1 Cor. 15:55).
- Personification is giving an object or idea human form or traits, as the writer of Proverbs does with "Wisdom" (Prov. 8 and 9).
- Hyperbole is exaggeration for effect: "You blind guides! You strain out a gnat but swallow a camel" (Matt. 23:24).
- Irony is saying the opposite of what you really mean, usually sarcastically, as when Elijah taunted the prophets of Baal because their god did not answer: "Shout louder! . . . Maybe he is sleeping and must be awakened" (1 Kings 18:27).

Poetic devices can be crucial to helping you understand the passage. The passage where Jesus says, "If your right hand causes you to sin, cut it off" (Matt. 5:30) is hyperbole. (It must be hyperbole; do you know anyone who ever followed that command literally?) If we see that command as exaggeration for effect, it emphasizes our Lord's concern that we avoid sin.

## DEALING WITH LONG PASSAGES

If you find it impossible to do this reading, rereading, and analyzing within a reasonable length of time, you probably are dealing with a long narrative passage. Find the portion of it that seems the most important, and concentrate your rereading and note-taking there.

You may also decide that the lesson contains too much Scripture, and you need to trim some out. That may seem like a radical concept, but remember that most lessons are deliberately designed with a lot of content, and if you have limited class time it is better to cover a few verses in depth than to skim several.

## STUDY THE CONTEXT

Now that you have read and reread the passage(s), look at the verses that precede and follow. Often you may need to read as much as a chapter or more prior to and after the passage you are studying to see how the verses fit in the context of the book. This is a very important step because the verses that precede or follow can often clarify an obscure point or put the teaching of a passage into perspective.

When I was in high school, I shared the following passage with a student teacher I had heard was interested in the Bible:

*What, after all, is Apollos? And what is Paul? Only servants, through whom you came to believe—as the Lord has assigned to each his task. I planted the seed, Apollos watered it, but God made it grow. So neither he who plants nor he who waters is anything, but only God, who makes things grow. (1 Cor. 3:5-7)*

"Yes, of course," she responded authoritatively. "The messenger is not important; it is the truth he or she teaches. Whether it is Paul, Apollos, Jesus, Buddha, Zoroaster, or anyone else, it's all the same. This is what the Bahai' faith teaches."

I had certainly opened a can of worms! But fortunately I had read the rest of the chapter and was able to point out that verses 10 and 11 contradicted her claim:

*By the grace God has given me, I laid a foundation as an expert builder, and someone else is building on it. But each one should be careful how he builds. For no one can lay any foundation other than the one already laid, which is Jesus Christ.*

At this, she sputtered a bit and said that one couldn't believe everything the Bible said.

"But you were perfectly willing to believe the Bible when it appeared to say what you wanted to hear," I answered. "If you read the Bible only to find support for your existing beliefs, how can you learn anything new?"

She was silent for a moment then turned and walked away. Thank God for the context!

By reading the context, you can usually get a better understanding of the passage's meaning. Another way to learn more about the passage is by seeing what the whole Bible has to say about it. Many study Bibles have references to related texts in the margins. You can also use a Bible concordance to look up passages on the same topic. Studying related passages is extremely important because so much Scripture makes reference to other parts of the Bible. Many events and teachings of the New Testament, for example, contain allusions to the Old Testament.

If a word continues to be repeated in the passages you look up, you may even want to do a study of that particular word and its deeper meaning. Some concordances are available that allow you to find out meanings and roots of words without having to learn the original languages of the Bible—Greek and Hebrew.

At this point, you should have learned enough about the passage to go to a commentary and see what other students of the Bible have to say. If you have done a thorough job of study, you may be surprised to find how much the commentary merely confirms your own conclusions. If, however, you find a definite conflict with your research and that of the commentator, be humble enough to make some revisions if necessary. But don't be too hasty to scrap your study results; commentators sometimes disagree with each other over the meaning of a passage!

Commentaries can be very helpful in bringing out historical, geographical, literary, and other aspects that will deepen your understanding. But avoid commentaries until you have completed your own Scripture research. George Sweeting warns us,

> Commentaries are splendid; however, beware of being chained to them. Someone has humorously said, "The Bible throws a lot of light on the commentaries." Any book which takes priority over the Bible becomes a crutch which leads to weakness. To read the words of men and neglect the Word of God is to say the books of men are of greater worth.[2]

This kind of in-depth study takes some time, but it can be pleasant and rewarding. All this work may also seem wasted when you realize that you cannot include all your research in the lesson. Some teachers are so anxious to share all that they have uncovered that the lesson gets bogged down in detail.

---

**Learn enough about the passage that you cannot include it all in the lesson. It adds depth to your lesson and will help you handle the unexpected question.**

---

Like an iceberg, with seven-eighths of its volume beneath the surface, your research should be more behind the scenes than stated outright. Learn enough about the passage that you cannot include it all in the lesson. It adds depth to your lesson and will help you handle the unexpected question. (For suggested Bible study resources, see Appendix A.)

## RETURNING TO THE LESSON

Now overlay your Scripture study and research onto the lesson in the teacher's guide. Does it fit? Is the main thrust of what you found in the Scripture passage the same as the main thrust of the lesson? Based on your study of the passage(s), you may conclude that it is necessary to make a major revision of the lesson aim, as well as much of the lesson's content.

An example at this point may be in order. A lesson for early elementary-age children on the feeding of the 5,000 may have a theme of sharing. Perhaps much will be made of the unnamed boy who shared his five loaves and two fish (John 6:9). But if you have done the kind of in-depth research described in this chapter, you will know that the main thrust of this passage is not that we should learn to share! Is it better (using this passage) to teach that sharing is good, or that Jesus had compassion on the crowds and provided for their physical needs?

Of course, we must keep in mind the age of the student. Any lesson we teach must be age-appropriate. Some subjects, though solidly biblical, are not appropriate for younger students, and some are far too complex. Often we must begin by teaching the simple truths and saving the more complex and in-depth issues for older students.

I cannot emphasize enough, however, that the Bible has to set the agenda for the lesson. As one writer puts it, "If someone desires to claim biblical authority for what he/she teaches, Scripture must be used only and always to teach what it intends to teach."[3] Moral principles such as sharing may be important to learn, but God has a deeper, more comprehensive plan for us in His Word—nothing less than spiritual transformation. If we use the Bible improperly to teach mere moralism, we weaken the authority of Scripture and give our students the impression that the Bible is nothing but a list of rules. On the contrary, the Bible is a book of spiritual revolution that can change the hearts and minds of students. If you are faithful to the integrity of the Word in your teaching, you will be a part of that spiritual transformation.

**THINKING IT OVER:**

1) Can you think of a time you questioned the way Scripture was used in a lesson plan?

2) Try the process of Scripture study described here on a familiar passage. What new insights did the process open up for you?

3) How can the message of the passage you have studied be taught to students at the age level you teach?

**MAKING IT WORK:**

Take the lesson you worked on in previous chapters and review its Scriptural foundation, especially as compared to the lesson aim. List a few other Scripture passages that could be used in conjunction with the lesson.

# <u>Notes</u>

# Chapter Five

# Hooks to Hang Truth On

LOOK AT THIS LESSON!" CHUCK CRIED. Joe and Mary were surprised; Chuck had never raised his voice in one of their meetings before. "It opens with a Bible story that three students are supposed to act out. None of the kids in my class are ever willing to do that sort of thing! Besides, the rest of the class has to sit tight until the 'drama team' gets ready."

"Chuck, you taught me not to see the lesson as set in stone," Mary said. "Why don't you just do something else?"

"I know, I know," Chuck replied. "But that's the problem; I can't come up with another idea. The well has gone dry." And to emphasize, he made an up-and-down motion as if operating the handle of an old farmhouse pump. Mary laughed.

"Chuck, I don't think your well has gone dry," Joe responded. "I just think you need something to prime the pump." And with that he started rooting through the black book bag he always seemed to carry with him. "Lemme see . . . it was here somewhere . . . Yes! I found it!" Joe pulled a dog-eared sheaf of papers out from the depths of the bag.

"This, my friend, is the answer you've been looking for," Joe cried triumphantly. "It's a list of teaching methods that I picked up at a Sunday school conference last year. It's never failed me yet!"

"What do you mean, 'teaching methods'?" Chuck asked skeptically, staring at the ragged list like it was some hideous creature that had just crawled out from under a rock.

"A method is just a way of presenting the content of the lesson," Joe replied, oblivious of Chuck's wrinkled nose and curling lip. "Let's look up 'dramatic methods' and see what we find."

Soon all three teachers were huddled over the list, and Chuck forgot all his initial doubts. "Hey, look—here's an idea: 'dramatic monologue.' Instead of having the kids act out the Bible story, I can dress up as a Bible character and tell the story that way."

"That's good, Chuck, but it cuts down class participation," Mary said. Chuck sighed, tossed the list down on the table, and began pacing back and forth aimlessly.

"Wait a minute, Chuck!" Joe had the list in his hand now, flipping the pages eagerly. "You can mix and match these ideas, y'know. Look at this one: 'Press Conference.' You dress up as the Bible character and hold a press conference—maybe even have some of the class ask prepared questions so you can stay on the topic. Do you think your students would go for that?"

"Are you kidding? They'll love it!" Chuck replied, the fire coming back into his eyes. "I'll bet a couple of guys will participate just to try to 'stump the teacher' or get me to step out of character, but that's all the better. I've just gotta be sure I really know that Bible story!"

---

**Methods are the container in which you carry the living water to your students.**

Methods are the container in which you carry the living water to your students. When you think of methods this way, you avoid the two opposite extremes of either minimizing the importance of methods (because without a "container" the water cannot get to the student) or thinking the method is the message. In this age of style over substance, we may be tempted to believe the Marshall McLuhan fallacy that "the medium is the message." The medium is not the message, but it affects the perception and comprehension of the message.

## LECTURE AND DISCUSSION

Lecture is the most over-used method by far. Continuing the "container" metaphor, lecture is a very big bucket, able to hold a lot of information. It is a flexible medium, useful for various age-groups, class sizes, and facilities. Speaking directly to your students is sometimes the easiest way to prepare and present certain material; it sometimes may appear to a teacher to be about the only way. Because it is so teacher-oriented, lecture may also appeal to one's ego. For these and other reasons, lecture is used far too often and in some of the most inappropriate ways.

Next on the list of over-used methods is group discussion. Because it fosters class participation and engages students' thinking, it is very attractive as a method. But when overused, discussion gets very predictable, with the teacher asking stock questions and students mouthing the answers they know we want to hear.

But class discussion can be an excellent way for students to correlate new information with what they already know. One way to start a class discussion in this direction is to ask a series of questions that begin with common knowledge and advance to new knowledge. Especially in adult classes, you may find this leads to asking questions for which you don't have an answer—or at least, not a complete one.

It can be helpful to write out the progression or series of questions before your class as part of your preparation. This is another form of teaching "with all your heart" because it can move a discussion into "uncharted territory." Then in faith, let it be an opportunity to let the Holy Spirit teach your students directly.

Jesus asked a pair of questions that led to a new discovery for His students. He asked His disciples, "Who do the people say that I am?" (Matt. 16:13). That question was easy; all the disciples had to do was repeat the rumors that were floating all around them. But then He asked a much harder, more personal question that advanced them to new knowledge: "Who do you say I am?" Peter's bold declaration, "You are the Christ, the Son of the living God," was a direct revelation from the Father, as Jesus Himself said (Matt. 16:15-17). Is it too much to think that the Holy Spirit may use a class discussion to lead one of your students to a similar epiphany?

Both lecture and discussion have their place; in fact, the next chapter will deal with them in more depth. But we should strive for creativity and variety in our teaching, and avoid the exclusive use of either lecture or discussion without incorporating other teaching methods with them. Any method can be overdone.

Because these two methods are so often used, some students know no other way to learn, and they can resist other methods. I once taught a senior adult class whose previous teacher had used only lecture. The students were accustomed to the teacher always talking; even the simplest group discussion was foreign to them. The first time I asked a question and tried to get a response, they looked at me as if I'd lost my mind. Some students thought my teaching approach was a bit radical; after all, a discussion in Sunday school was almost like interrupting the pastor in the middle of his sermon! But eventually a few students began participating, and over the next several weeks, they even became willing to try a few other methods, such as writing exercises and small-group discussions.

---

**The skillful weaving of lecture and discussion with other teaching methods contributes to a lively and creative classroom atmosphere.**

---

If you define *lecture* as any time you make a statement to the class and *group discussion* as any time you solicit a response from the class, it is hard to imagine a lesson without the use of these two tools. It is when they become your only tools that you are in danger of putting your class to sleep. The skillful weaving of lecture and discussion with other teaching methods contributes to a lively and creative classroom atmosphere.

## CATEGORIES OF TEACHING METHODS

A list of various methods is included in Appendix B, with advantages, disadvantages, and tips for use. The different methods may seem almost endless, yet according to Marlene LeFever, they fall into three basic categories, reflecting three different ways or combinations of learning:

1) Visual, such as object lessons or art projects; students who like these kinds of methods learn best by seeing.

2) Auditory, including lecture and discussion; students who like these kinds of methods learn best by hearing.

3) Tactile-Kinesthetic, encompassing various activities; students who like these kinds of methods learn best by moving.[1]

Some methods span more than one of these categories. Strive to choose methods that will enable you to reach visual, auditory, and tactile-kinesthetic learners all at the same time or at different times throughout the lesson. One of the ways to accomplish this is by mixing methods.

## MIXING METHODS

The very best methods do not always fit neatly into a single category—or to put it another way, they are a combination of several methods. The best example I have ever seen came from a young man from Africa named Alexi. He attended a Sunday school teachers' training class taught by missionary Lorinda Robinson, but when it came time for the students to conduct a sample lesson before the class, Alexi wanted to bow out. He was afraid he could not come up with a creative idea. After Lorinda encouraged Alexi to ask the Lord for help, she tells what happened:

> On the last day of classes, the students have to teach their object lessons. I was anxious to see what Alexi would do. When his turn finally came, he stood up and pulled a beautiful, brand-new, white-as-snow handkerchief out of his pocket.
>
> "Whew, it's hot today," he said. "Some of you look like you're perspiring. Would one of you like to use my new handkerchief to wipe your face?"
>
> Several hands went up and the handkerchief was passed around. Finally Alexi took it back. Then he dropped it on the ground and stepped on it, grinding it into the dirt! Picking up the dirty handkerchief, he asked, "Now who wants to use my handkerchief?"
>
> Not a hand was raised.

He asked, "Why don't you want to use my handkerchief anymore? You wanted to use it a minute ago. It's the same handkerchief."

The students all answered, "Because it's dirty."

Alexi continued, "What would make you want to use it again?"

Someone answered, "It would have to be clean."

On hearing this, Alexi produced a bucket of water and began to rinse the handkerchief. While he rinsed, he talked.

"You know, we're like this handkerchief. When God made man, man was without sin. He was pure, just like the handkerchief was clean when it was new. But when man chose to sin, he was no longer pure. Just like we don't want to put a dirty handkerchief on our faces, sin can't enter into the presence of a holy God. Let's look at our handkerchief now."

Taking the handkerchief out of the bucket, he asked, "Is it clean now?"

It wasn't.

"Why not?" he asked.

The students knew the answer to the question. "You didn't use any soap!" they said.

So Alexi produced a little laundry detergent and began to wash the handkerchief. As he washed, he sang:

What can wash away my sin?
Nothing but the blood of Jesus.
What can make me whole again?
Nothing but the blood of Jesus.

"You know," he said, "just like we needed more than

water to clean the handkerchief, we need more than good deeds to be pure in God's eyes. Jesus died so we could be reconciled to God. He made us pure so He could use us. If God were to look at your spiritual heart, what would He see—a heart dirty with sin or one that's clean because you've asked Jesus to forgive you of your sin?"

When Alexi sat down, the students broke into applause. Finally one of his friends asked him, "Where did you get that object lesson?"

"God gave it to me," Alexi replied.[2]

Alexi's story was an example of an object lesson—or was it? If you look closely, you can see that Alexi used lecture, class discussion, demonstration, and even music in his presentation—as well as an object lesson!

Many teaching methods are never stand-alone; they must be used in conjunction with other methods. Can you imagine, for example, bringing an object to class and not using lecture or class discussion to explain its significance?

Teaching methods may vary, but the teacher who can hold the interest of the students is leading them into unexpected areas of learning. As this takes place, each student is learning in his or her own particular way. Even when students are simply listening to a story, they are participating through listening.

## METHODS AND THE THREE-POINT OUTLINE

Another thing Alexi's lesson teaches is the fact that a method can be used to span more than one section of the three-point outline. It can even comprise the entire lesson. While the three-point outline is easy to remember and very flexible, don't let it force you into always using separate teaching methods, one for each section. This can work well with the right transitions (which will be discussed in the next chapter), but you need to avoid the compartmentalization and predictability that can happen when three or four very different methods are used separately.

Some of the best lessons have steps that are obvious only to the teacher. If you analyze Alexi's lesson, for example, you can discern a beginning, middle, and end, but it is very subtle and smooth.

It is true, however, that certain teaching methods are most effective as part of the introduction, while others are better suited for the body or conclusion.

* A high-activity method works very well at the beginning of the lesson because it grabs attention. Such a method could be continued through the body of the lesson, or it could transition into a method with a more moderate activity level. Finally the conclusion would be a lower activity level method so that the students can think through what they have done in class.

* As I said earlier, lecture is a "big bucket," a high-information method. Certain other methods—crafts, games, drama—are more low-information. This does not mean that they are not as useful, but they may not always fit the body of the lesson, which is typically high-information. Low-information methods can be very useful in introducing a lesson where they effectively "set the stage" by a dramatic presentation of the lesson's main theme. However, there are times when the students may participate in an activity or make a craft of an actual Bible object that will help them understand the meaning of the lesson at a new level. Because of the discussion that accompanies the activity or craft, it can have high student participation and rich content as well.

* If a certain teaching method is relatively complex to prepare and

present, or if you have never tried it before, it may be best to use it to introduce the lesson. Then if it doesn't seem to work, you have time to switch gears and move on to the rest of the lesson. If you use such a method to conclude the lesson and it doesn't fly, you run the risk of having students leave the class without having a clear idea of what they have learned.

In choosing methods for your lessons, it is critical to keep in mind the age-group you are teaching. Of course, you cannot use methods with toddlers that involve reading or writing, and the senior adult class may be too sedentary for a high-energy activity! But there are issues that are less obvious, such as attention span, social development, level of responsibility, regularity of attendance, etc., which vary from age to age, and make different methods either more or less practical for your class. These are issues that relate to customizing the lesson. A teacher must have a good understanding of the physical, emotional, social, mental, and spiritual characteristics that are unique to the age group he or she is teaching. The teacher also needs to become well acquainted with the individual students in the class. If you do this, the appropriateness of a particular method for your class should become obvious.

Some methods are full-class activities while others are small-group or individual. Some appeal to artistic students, thinkers, or active learners. A variety of teaching methods is the key to keeping your students' interest and reaching every one of them. There are so many kinds of methods that you could try something new every week for a year and not exhaust the list. And when you consider the various ways that you can combine different methods, the possibilities are endless!

**THINKING IT OVER:**

1) How often do you use lecture and discussion in your teaching?

2) What other methods, whether listed in Appendix B or not, have you tried and found success with?

3) What methods are listed in Appendix B that you have never used? Try one of them in your next lesson.

**MAKING IT WORK:**

Take the lesson you worked on in previous chapters and incorporate at least three teaching methods from Appendix B—one for each step of the lesson. Identify ways you could mix together at least two methods from the list in the Appendix B.

# <u>Notes</u>

# Chapter Six

# The Words
# of Your Mouth

ONE HOUR AND TWENTY MINUTES INTO THE INDUSTRIAL TRAINING SESSION, JOE COULD STAND NO MORE. His boss had insisted that he and his installation crew attend this class, but so far he could find little of it that related to his job. It irritated him that the instructor seemed to be more concerned with completing a prepared spiel than explaining how the new equipment was to be installed.

*If he puts up one more meaningless wiring diagram on that overhead, I'm going to throw up,* Joe said to himself. It occurred to him, however, that gagging would not produce the desired results, so he contented himself with asking a question that he hoped would bring the topic down to street level.

The instructor seemed puzzled by Joe's raised hand, but he nodded in his direction, and Joe stood up to speak.

"I take it you've installed a number of these systems."

"Why, yes. Why do you ask?"

"I'd like to know . . . well, what's the hardest installation you ever did?"

"What? What do you want to know that for?" The instructor looked at him like he was crazy, and Joe began to turn a light shade of crimson.

"Well, I mean . . . it's just that we've had nothing but theory all morning. I'd like to hear how it applies in real life." After a moment of silence, several of his co-workers joined in a slow, steady round of applause—the response of a crowd whose patience had been sorely tried.

Now it was the instructor's turn to step our of his "comfort zone." Joe had to admit, however, that the poor guy took it in stride. From that point on, the seminar was a lot more lively and informative.

As he started to prepare his Sunday school lesson, Joe thought back on his experience in the seminar. *How many times have I bored my students to tears?* He thought, *Am I all theory and no practical application?* Joe decided from then on to make sure he included real-life examples and other elements in his lesson to grab and hold the students' attention.

* * * * *

Diogenes is said to have wandered through the marketplace of an ancient Greek city in the middle of the day, carrying a lighted lantern over his head and peering about intently. When the curiosity of the townspeople had reached its peak, they asked what he was doing. He replied, "I am looking for an honest man."

Diogenes was a consummate teacher. His silent playacting made his point, but he didn't teach anyone anything until he opened his mouth. It may be possible to teach without speaking, but I haven't found a way yet.

It is a teacher's duty to be interesting, said Augustine.[1] And making your teaching interesting begins with the words that come from your mouth. Whether you are asking or answering questions, leading a discussion, lecturing, or transitioning from one section of the lesson to another, the momentum and interest level of your students depend on your words.

"Woe is me!" you say. "If my students' attention depends on my words, then I am undone, for my speech is uncouth, and I am a dullard at social events!"

Perhaps you wouldn't say it quite that way, but you get the idea. Fortunately, there are a number of simple techniques you can use to keep minds from wandering and eyelids from drooping.

## A "QUESTION-ABLE" STRATEGY

To lead a discussion, prop up a sagging lecture, or introduce a new subject, the ancient but still effective practice of asking questions is invaluable. The mental stimulation of questions often brings out the best in your students. Good questions are gold, and the best teachers know it.

The greatest teachers in the world were known for their questions. Socrates taught his students almost exclusively through the use of questions. (Talk about a guy who was stuck on a single teaching method!) The apostle Paul asked questions all the time, even in his letters!

Jesus did more than anyone with questions. He used them to make a point (Matt. 22:20), to challenge (Matt. 20:22), to rectify a misunderstanding (Mark 8:17-21), and even to rebuke (Matt. 14:31)

---

**Good questions help students discover truth
for themselves.**

Remember that questions are meant to guide your students along a pattern of thinking. But there's a difference between guiding and herding. Good questions help students discover truth for themselves. Bad questions take students along the same tired old ruts to an obvious conclusion.

This is the very problem with questions in a few teacher's guides and Bible studies: obvious answers with trite conclusions. Even worse are the discussion questions which lead to no conclusions at all and end up leading students in circles. Don't fool yourself into asking questions just to fill time. Better to ask no questions at all!

If your questions are going to take the class in the right direction, they need to be in the right kind of progression:

- Concrete questions that lead into abstract ones.
- Yes/no questions that lead into critical ones.
- Objective questions that lead into subjective ones.
- Fact-finding questions that lead into analytical ones.

For example, in a narrative passage of the Bible you might begin by asking a number of questions related to the details of the story, possibly listing the details on a chalkboard or newsprint. As the data grows in volume, switch to fewer questions aimed at interpreting the information. Finally, wind up the question-and-answer session with one or two questions to help apply the truths to life.

Other patterns of questioning include:

1) G.O.A.T. ( Goal, Obstacles, Answers, Time): Ask the students to find the goal of a certain passage, character, or biblical author. Then ask what obstacles are encountered in reaching that goal. Inquire as to what answers the author or character found to overcome the obstacle. Finally, ask the students to identify how this drama played out chronologically over time.

2) Problem/solution: Ask questions that identify a problem, and

then compare alternatives. Have Scripture available that speaks to the issue, but do not be too quick to share. Perhaps the students will come up with their own Scripture for the solution.

3) Analysis of Bible passage: Inquire as to the background, setting, theme, "big idea," repeated words and phrases, and related Scripture passages. As with problem/solution, research the passage beforehand, but keep that information in your "back pocket" and occasionally "seed" the conversation with the facts you have gathered.

4) Contrast: Pair up contrasting questions. Jesus used this method when he quizzed His disciples in Matthew 16:13 and 15: "Who do people say the Son of Man is? . . . Who do you say I am?" The Lord's contrasting questions provided the Holy Spirit with the opportunity to plant in Peter's mind the revelation of Jesus' true nature: "You are the Christ, the Son of the living God" (Matt. 16:16). Contrast can be an excellent way to help your students see subtleties of truth.

5) Lists: Get your students to compile all that they know about the subject at hand. In other words, ask, "What are some of the aspects of [the topic]?" After you have listed (usually on a chalkboard or newsprint) the various aspects of the issue, you can then discuss how they are interrelated. Avoid asking for specific numbers in a list question, such as "What are the five commands in this passage?" Someone is bound to come up with a sixth one! Besides, you are telling your class that you have an agenda, and you aren't going to leave this question until all five commands are found. That gets old fast.

Some teachers are fond of the "devil's advocate" approach: asking questions that reflect a negative or anti-biblical viewpoint to get students to look at a truth in a new way. While it has its place, the name of this method is appropriate because it can backfire. Often the questions generated by "devil's advocate" have no easy answers and reflect controversies that theologians have grappled with for centuries, such as, "Why would a loving God allow suffering?" The "devil's advocate" method can get a discussion moving to new ground when it's in a rut. But it can also stifle a lively discussion or introduce confusion into a class on the verge of making a discovery. Use it, but only judiciously and wisely.

Adapt your questions to various age levels. Younger children will be more comfortable with concrete questions while older students may like to do more abstract thinking. Some older kids respond well to hypothetical questions such as "How would you feel if . . . ?" or "What would you think if . . . ?", but with younger kids who are at the "let's pretend" stage, you need to ask questions that will stir up their imagination.

## WHAT ABOUT WHEN STUDENTS ASK QUESTIONS?

---

**Though a question may be unexpected, it must never be unwelcome. It can be an opportunity for you to step back and clarify a part of the lesson that several of the students had trouble following.**

---

With experience, you can learn to anticipate questions from students and even plan for them. Though a question may be unexpected, it must never be unwelcome. It can be an opportunity for you to step back and clarify a part of the lesson that several of the students had trouble following. So be thankful for questions; they may interrupt your train of thought or slow down the pace of the class, but they can also help get all the students on the same page.

"There are no foolish questions," the great scientist Charles

Steinmetz said, "and no man becomes a fool until he stops asking questions."[2] There are some questions, however, that are tough for teachers to deal with. Here are two of my favorite puzzlers:

1) "WHY?" This is especially typical of younger children. Some questions, especially those that involve God's character, nature, and motivations, are very difficult. Why does God love us? Why can't we see God? It is okay to say "I don't know," even to the youngest child. When we admit that we don't know everything, we acknowledge that God is bigger and smarter than we are, and the students can begin to get a bigger picture of who God is.

2) "How does this relate to [my hobby horse]?" (Of course, they don't put it that way, but it is the essence of what they mean!) This is a question often asked by younger adults. A student may have a pet peeve about legalism, for example. You can teach about the Sermon on the Mount, Noah and the ark, or Christ's Second Coming, and that student will find a way to relate it to the issue of legalism so that he can deliver his standard campaign speech against it. This can be tolerated to a certain extent, but if it becomes repetitive and disruptive, you may have to gently squelch it by answering their question with a question: "How does this relate to the topic under discussion?" All but the most insensitive student will recognize that he or she is taking the discussion off on a tangent.

## STUDENT DISCUSSION TYPES (for Upper Elementary age children through Adult)

Different types of students emerge in a discussion session.

### 1) The Talker

At his worst, he only likes to hear the sound of his own voice; at his best, he can be an expressive and responsive student. His aggressive participation may scare off other students, but on the other hand, his willingness to share may encourage others to add their comments.

## 2) The Arguer

He looks for conflict and disagreement and wants to "win" all the time. Such a student may cause problems but can also stimulate discussion and force others to think through the implications of an issue. Sometimes a little controversy can be good!

## 3) The Peacemaker

He tries to resolve disagreements and reconcile opposing opinions. This can be an admirable trait, but it can also stifle discussion and prevent a class from getting past the superficial.

## 4) The Clam

This is the person who doesn't say anything. This kind of behavior really bothers some teachers who think that every student needs to participate as much as the others. The quiet ones, however, often take in a lot more than those who talk a lot. It doesn't hurt to invite the quieter ones to join in the conversation, but don't push too hard.

## 5) The Eclectic

His brain is always riding on the ragged edge. This person's contributions may take the discussion off on a tangent or introduce a new aspect to the issue being discussed, one that no one else (including the teacher) would have thought of.

None of these different types is always bad, but the dangers are obvious as one or more of them can take control of a discussion. It doesn't matter what type of student takes control; the discussion dies when anyone, even the teacher, dominates the conversation.

Why, then, do we need to know about the different types? The better we know them, the better we are able to help them release control without causing them embarrassment, offense, or pain. We need to vary our strategy for dealing with each type.

## FIGHTING THE FEAR OF PARTICIPATION

In the previous chapter I mentioned a senior adult class which rebelled at participating. Students who are used to lecture are typically intimidated by attempts to make them participate. If no one ever speaks out in class, it's very tough to be the first. But students who are afraid to speak up can often be weaned away from their fear by individual assignments which are then discussed by the whole class. A more traditional method of discussion asks for spontaneous responses, but a class that is used to the teacher saying everything will fall silent when asked to participate. Individual (usually written) assignments can give the students something to talk about.

For example, you could have the class read a passage of Scripture and ask them to write down "at least three things that Jesus did," "the words that are repeated in the passage," or "how the different characters reacted to the situation." After a few minutes, you can ask for students to respond and write their answers on the board. Because they have already written down their answers, students will often have no qualms about sharing their insights, and your positive feedback will reinforce them.

Even if you still get no verbal response, you can turn the discussion time into a class "survey" by asking such questions as, "How many of you wrote down that Jesus wrote in the sand?" and count the hands that are raised. After a few questions, ask if anyone wrote down an answer that has not yet been mentioned. When I tried this method on the senior adult class, it was almost as if a dam had burst; previously silent and stone-faced students jumped in to be the first to have their say, and the discussion was quite lively, comparatively speaking.

## ILLUSTRATIONS AND QUOTATIONS

Using illustrations is an effective form of the lecture method. Putting these "word pictures" into your students' minds can help them remember the truths you are teaching long after the class is over. If used in the introduction, a good illustration can be continually referred to throughout the lesson to weave a thread of continuity into your presentation. A lesson can also be concluded with an anecdotal illustration to show a practical life application in the lesson.

It is important, however, that an illustration clearly communicates the message without including a lot of unnecessary details that contradict or confuse the message.

I saw one example of how confusion could happen in a lesson plan I was editing. Describing the sandalwood tree, the lesson read as follows:

> Under the right conditions, a [sandalwood] seed on the ground will burst and send down a root into another tree. Then, as a parasite, it draws its strength from the other tree until its roots are sufficient to support itself in the extremely hot climate.
>
> This story illustrates a principle for Christians. New Christians should attach themselves to strong Christians while sending down "roots" into the Word.[3]

This is an excellent illustration, except for one thing: the phrase "as a parasite" in the second sentence adds a negative connotation to what should be a very positive concept. Needless to say, we didn't want to make young Christians feel like parasites, so we deleted that phrase from the lesson!

With younger children especially, it is important that an illustration be free of ambiguity. Even with adults, contradictory wording tends to blunt the edge of the illustration. If you have the opportunity, try out an illustration on a few people before using it in class. Ask for their honest opinions, and learn to develop a thick skin. Look for someone with a good sense of humor; there's nothing worse than an unintentionally humorous illustration . . . except the illustration that's supposed to be funny, but only offends or confuses.

A provocative quotation can also spark a lively discussion, provide an effective transition from one portion of the lesson to another, or be used as a wrap-up for the conclusion of the lesson. Whether serious, humorous, profound, or ironic, the right quotation can add a dash of spice to any lecture or discussion. With older teens or adults, you may even want to use a quotation from a critic of Christianity or the Bible, as a contrast. But like the "devil's advocate" questions, practice this sparingly and with wisdom.

Quotations are effective with younger children as well, though they should usually take the form of a poem or song. Rhyme and music help the younger child fix the quotation in his or her mind, while older students do not always need these kinds of memory techniques.

---

**You can buy books of illustrations and quotations, but it is often more effective to draw from your personal reading or your own life experiences.**

---

You can buy books of illustrations and quotations, but it is often more effective to draw from your personal reading or your own life experiences. Imagine a teacher who is teaching a lesson on God's comfort in times of grief. She has the opportunity to tell the story of a famous Christian whose spouse died or the story of her own grief when she lost her husband three years ago. Which do you think would be the most effective?

## TRUSTING GOD FOR OUR WORDS

Above all, we should completely depend on the Lord for the words we use before our students. Only He can infuse confidence and authority into what we say. Peter counsels us, "If anyone speaks, he should do it as one speaking the very words of God" (1 Pet. 4:11). When bathed in prayerful study, this can be our experience.

**THINKING IT OVER:**

1) On a scale of 1 to 10, how interesting do you think you are as a teacher?

2) What was the most difficult situation you've had with a student during a discussion? Did he or she fit one of the types? How did you handle the situation? What would you do differently, looking back?

3) Do you pray for God to anoint your words? Remember to ask for this specifically the next time you teach.

**MAKING IT WORK:**

Using one of the patterns of questioning listed in this chapter, take the lesson you worked on in previous chapters and prepare a list of discussion questions for it.

# <u>Notes</u>

# Chapter Seven

# It's Show Time!

WITH HELP FROM JOE AND CHUCK, NOT TO MENTION A LOT OF PRAYER, MARY HAD LEARNED TO REFOCUS HER PREPARATION TIME TO MAKE THE LESSON HER OWN AND TO KEEP AN OUTLINE IN HER HEAD. Though she felt more confident and noticed the students were more attentive, she still tended to keep her nose stuck in the teacher's guide throughout the lesson. *This is so silly,* she said to herself. *I really don't need a "security blanket" anymore.*

One Sunday morning, she stood in front of her class and opened the teacher's guide. The title of the lesson leaped out at her: "Trusting God." *Do you really trust Me?* the Lord spoke to her heart. Mary closed the teacher guide, with the lesson bookmarked—just in case she needed a quick reminder. Then, putting on her best smile, she began leading the class in their memory verse: "In God I trust; I will not be afraid" (Ps. 56:11).

\* \* \* \* \*

So far, we have discussed preparing a lesson. This chapter will deal with presenting a lesson. But first, let's review the steps involved in customizing a standard lesson plan:

1) *Lesson "deconstruction":* To customize your teaching, it is necessary to "deconstruct" the standardized lesson, breaking it down into identifiable parts and analyzing what the curriculum writer is trying to accomplish. This is not a veiled attempt to alter the content of the lesson; it is an overt attempt to rework the presentation of the material so that it flows from you in a natural and easy-going manner. By listing the Scripture passages, teaching methods, teaching objectives (stated and unstated), and other components of the lesson plan, you are laying the groundwork for reconstructing the lesson into a customized format.

2) *Research:* Through your analysis, you may discover "holes" in the lesson plan or unpursued aspects of the topic being taught. Are there other Scriptures that come into play? What have great Christian writers said about the subject? Like the original curriculum writer, you may find it necessary to leave out some parts from the actual lesson. But having done the research, you won't be flustered when someone has a question about a point not directly covered in the lesson. Research may help you see the subject in a new light as well. And last but not least, your own Bible study may reveal the need to adjust parts of the lesson to conform to the central theme of the passage.

3) *Pattern Reconstruction:* From your analysis of the lesson and your research, a pattern should begin to emerge. What aspect of the topic should be emphasized? How could that aspect be introduced? Is there a concluding thought that would help the student apply this truth? Prepare an outline with a three-point format. Choose one or more teaching methods for each section of the lesson. Prepare notes for the lesson in an outline such as the following:

Aim: _____

Scripture: _____

   Step One: _____

      Method: _____

      Props: _____

      Transition: _____

         Estimated Time: _____

   Step Two: _____

      Method: _____

      Props: _____

      Transition: _____

         Estimated Time: _____

   Step Three: _____

      Method: _____

      Props: _____

      Transition: _____

         Estimated Time: _____

*4) Final Preparation:* Walk yourself through the lesson, making sure that all your details are covered, all "props" are available, and all transitions are clear. Are you having second thoughts about any particular activity (you don't think you can pull it off, the students wouldn't like it, or there isn't time to do it)? What could replace it? Plan for disruptions and talkative students. Leave time for questions. Get a good night's sleep.

## LESSON PRESENTATION

_____

**This is the main purpose of the three-step format:**

**to create a structure for the lesson that is simple and natural enough that you can teach from memory.**

---

Now that you have prepared the lesson, how do you present it? The preparation you have done and the time you have spent in prayer should encourage you. And since the three-point outline (Introduction, Body, and Conclusion) is easy to remember, you should be able to teach in front of your students without being overly-dependent on any notes or even the teacher's guide. This is the main purpose of the three-point outline: to create a structure for the lesson that is simple and natural enough that you can teach mostly from memory.

Certainly, you can prepare notes to help structure your thoughts and aid in memorization, but you should refer to them as little as possible during class. If you become completely lost, you can refer to them, but consider it a last resort.

Teaching without repeatedly referring to notes is not merely an exercise for daredevils. It has some distinct advantages:

*1) It is an exercise in faith.* You have prayed and prepared for your class. This method is a way of trusting God to guide you as you teach.

*2) It brings spontaneity and naturalness to your presentation.* If you make little use of notes, you are less likely to sound like you are reading in a monotone from the teacher's guide. Your explanations and transitions will have natural phrasing and tone and will therefore be easier to listen to and understand.

*3) It will encourage you to prepare better.* Without something to read from in front of the class, you instinctively begin to plan out how to introduce this or that activity or what you will say if someone asks a question. By combining this "what-if" planning with an ability to think on your feet, you will be prepared for just about anything that happens in class.

4) *It is exciting and challenging.* Teaching with a very loose grip on your notes or a teacher's guide can seem scary, but you can make it work to your advantage. Just as an actor learns to cope with stage jitters and uses it to strengthen his delivery, you can allow that minor tension to keep you alert and focused on the task of teaching.

Comparing a teacher to an actor is a useful metaphor for Sunday school. Although the task of a teacher is not merely to entertain, teaching is like performing, in that it attempts to gain and hold the attention of an audience. As a teacher, you are always "on stage." Knowing what works for your students and knowing the content of your material are keys to your success, just as "playing to the audience" and knowing one's lines are critical to an actor's success. Your success can be determined by how you deliver your lines, but also by what you wear, how you stand and gesture, and your staging and props. For more insight into this relationship, see the book *Teaching and Performing.*[1]

You, the teacher, have a big advantage over the actor, however. While an actor has a script written by someone else, your "script" is written by you alone, and you have the freedom to alter it as you wish. If you worry about how you will remember your introduction, transitions, and instructions for the class, keep working on the wording until it is easy to remember. It is no coincidence that well-worded statements are referred to as "memorable." But be sure to prepare for the unpredictable event—a question, an interruption, or the late student. The interruption should not keep you from a successful lesson. By remembering your three-point plan, you should be able to easily get back to the lesson no matter what has happened to interrupt the flow.

Do you remain unconvinced? It may seem reckless to teach

without detailed notes, but if you have never prepared for a class using the three-point outline, you are in for a surprise. Your advance preparation and familiarity with the lesson should help you to naturally convey the truth. Your lesson will become more like a conversation than a lecture, more like a sharing of ideas among friends than a question-and-answer session. "The teacher must not simply know the lesson," Luther Allan Weigle contends, "he must know it in such a way that he can cause others to know it."[2]

## TIME FOR ALL THINGS

---

**If on Sunday morning your carefully planned schedule is altered by unexpected circumstances, don't be discouraged. Such unplanned events also happened to Jesus when He was teaching.**

---

One of the biggest items you have to juggle during the lesson is the time you have to teach. Without careful planning, the first step that you expected to take a few minutes can eat up most of the period, leaving little room for the rest of the lesson. This is just one of the advantages of a "dry run" of the lesson sometime before Sunday. Walk through the lesson, performing the activities and keeping track of the time. You may find it necessary to alter or eliminate an activity because of the amount of time it takes. If on Sunday morning your carefully planned schedule is altered by unexpected circumstances, don't be discouraged. Such apparently unplanned events also happened to Jesus when He was teaching.

## TIME KILLERS AND HOW TO AVOID THEM

Any activity that is not actual teaching or learning should not be allowed to intrude on valuable class time. Attendance, offering, announcements, new student registration, worksheet distribution, etc., may be necessary, but they can be big time wasters. You can cut non-learning time to a minimum through the proper preparation:

1) *Ask students to participate.* Even in a preschool class, a student can at least collect the offering. Pass around the attendance sheet rather than filling it out yourself, or have a student be responsible for attendance.

2) *Prepare packets for group activities.* If part of the lesson involves dividing into groups of three and writing your thoughts on certain Scripture passages, prepare several packets with three Bibles, three writing pads, and three pencils. This preparation can help avoid the delays caused by students scrambling to find all the needed materials.

3) *Don't waste time debating discipline with a student.* Find a way to lovingly but firmly restore order; then get on with the lesson.

4) *Encourage one-sentence prayers.* A common practice is to pray in a circle or in small groups with each student praying for a single request in a single sentence.

5) *Get to the classroom early.* Make sure all the chairs are set up, and all props and materials are ready.

6) *Clean up later.* If it is possible, leave the room as-is and clean up after the service or the next day.

The issue of keeping an eye on the clock brings up the question of whether all the steps of the lesson should be given the same amount of time. Students' learning styles, because they relate to different sections in the outline, tend to favor "equal time." That would mean that the body of the lesson, which tends to focus on two learning styles (analytical and common-sense), should be about twice as long as either the introduction or conclusion. Each learner should be given a chance to learn in his or her own style as much as possible. Giving a lesson the proper pacing is very important.

Your own learning style may come into play at this point. Do you find yourself rushing through the introduction in order to get to the Bible content (your favorite part of the lesson)? Or do you rush through the introduction and body of the lesson to get to the conclusion? Be careful that your own learning style does not become the primary driving force in the lesson. Maintain a healthy balance and address all four learning styles throughout the lesson.

Be sensitive to your students and their level of comprehension. Learn to be a reader of their faces. If they are smiling and attentive, your pacing of the lesson is probably okay. If they seem confused or bored, you may need to slow down or speed up! Watch the clock, but do not be a slave to it. If the class seems ready for the body of the lesson after 10 minutes, don't stretch out step one just to fit your schedule. Also, if a concept seems hard to understand, it is better to make sure your students understand before moving on, and let the conclusion be slightly perfunctory, rather than allowing students to leave class without having absorbed the content at all.

And finally, it may sometimes be appropriate to drop your prepared lesson in favor of a compelling need, a complex question, or a puzzling problem raised by one or more students. The class may be devastated by the unexpected loss of one of their members; they may be preoccupied by the recent resignation of the youth pastor; or one or more students may be asking questions about salvation. Only the most rigid and insensitive teacher would try to continue with a prepared lesson in these situations!

Mavis Weidman puts it this way: "You know that there may be the occasional time when your plans may be set aside because an unforeseen need arises which must be met. After all, you are teaching pupils, not quarterlies; you are changing lives, not covering a lesson; you are guiding your pupils into discovering truth, not giving a prescribed lecture."[3]

**THINKING IT OVER:**

1) Prepare a lesson plan using the three-point outline (Introduction, Body, and Conclusion). How is it different from the way you have prepared lessons in the past?

2) How do think your presentation may differ from the lessons you have presented in the past?

3) What are some of your biggest time wasters? How do you handle them?

**MAKING IT WORK:**

Take the lesson you worked on in previous chapters and finish any final "tweaks," then take it through a "dry run." Determine any areas that may be awkward or slow, and rework them so that you can teach it smoothly.

# Chapter Eight

# Monday-Morning Hindsight

As the students filed out of his classroom, Joe had mixed feelings about the lesson he had just taught. While it ended quite well, he had a hard time getting the class started and keeping them on the topic. And that small-group exercise seemed to have its awkward moments. *I haven't got time to think about this now,* he thought, *I'll just jot down some notes about it.* And before heading to the sanctuary for the morning worship service, he wrote down his impressions of what went right and wrong that morning.

Later, Joe stopped a few of his students and asked what they thought. It took some convincing to persuade them that he was doing more than fishing for compliments, but finally they gave him their honest opinion: the introduction to the topic was confusing, and the small-group exercise that followed was uncomfortable and embarrassing for them because no one knew where the lesson was going. "I thought it was just me that was confused," Jared said. "But once the others admitted that they were in the dark too, I didn't feel so bad!"

One of the kids said she thought the exercise was some kind of test to see how the students could work together with ambiguous information. "I was really disappointed to find that we had just missed the point!" All the students said that the confusion was cleared up by the end of the class, however.

What went wrong? Joe was more curious than upset over this question, so Monday he got up early to review his lesson plan and teaching notes just to see if he could find the snag. Joe didn't realize he was doing evaluation; all he knew was that he had done something wrong in teaching the lesson, and he was bound and determined to find out what it was so he could avoid doing it again.

\* \* \* \* \*

*Evaluation:* it's easy to talk about, but how often is it really done? Many people put it up there with cleaning the back seat of the car. It's something we know we ought to do, but we never seem to get around to it.

One of the main stumbling blocks is that we lack a real reason for doing evaluation. Why rehash our failures? Why try to dissect our successes? On the one hand, we are afraid to relive the pain; on the other hand, we don't want to jinx our good fortune. It's no good hearing the old saying that we learn from our mistakes; as Charlie Brown said, "That makes me the smartest person in the world!"

But evaluation has a practical side. It's the first step in preparing next week's lesson! Why?

1) *Every lesson should be a successor to the previous one.* When we evaluate what the students have learned, we know how to pick up where we left off.

2) *The only way to learn from a mistake is to apply what you've learned*

*to the very next lesson.* Like getting back on the horse that threw you, you have a chance to break the cycle of failure—or at least learn how to sidestep it.

*3) It gives you an opportunity to capitalize on your successes.* Only by evaluating what went right in the most recent class can you hope to keep that momentum going. Can you repeat a success without making all your lessons come out the same? If so, it's a great feeling. Two home run lessons in a row can make you feel that all your trouble was worth it.

*4) Finally, keeping the next week's lesson in mind forces you to be simple and practical.* No room for theory here. You want to know what went right so you can capitalize on it next time. You also want to know what went wrong so you can avoid another application of egg on the face.

---

**When you evaluate, you get to see patterns. You avoid becoming a tape recorder.**

---

When you evaluate, you get to see patterns. You avoid becoming a tape recorder. That's the danger in customizing curriculum—all your lessons can start to sound the same. But when you evaluate, you prevent the "parrot syndrome."

So how do you evaluate? The key is to get feedback from your students. You can get feedback by asking directly. Also, as you get to know your students, you can learn how to read them during the class.

## IN-CLASS EVALUATION

One type of evaluation is done during the lesson. Make sure the lesson aim is clear and measurable; then use it as a signpost to help you stay on track. In other words, at various points throughout the lesson, do a quick (maybe a second or two) evaluation: are they following this so far?

For example, to teach a lesson on justification, you start with introducing the lesson. At the end of the introduction, you pause for a second (literally) and ask yourself, "Does the class know what our topic is? Have I got them thinking about justification? Are they at least starting to have a clear definition of it in their minds?" You can even take time to actually review the material you have just covered with the students to see if they are on track. If it appears to be so, go on. If not, continue the introduction as you reiterate what you want them to be thinking about. It may be that all they learn that day is a definition of the word "justification," but it's better than learning nothing.

What if some are following you and others aren't? Ask those who appear to understand if they can put into their own words what has been learned so far. This often gives other students a chance to catch up.

## STUDENT EVALUATION

Teachers always say that feedback is important to help students learn, but that isn't the only reason teachers like feedback. Class participation and discussion helps the teacher see if the message is getting across. Be honest with your class. Tell them that you need to know if they are following the lesson before you can go on to the next point. Students have no problem giving feedback if they know why. Most students rebel against feedback if they think you're trying to get them to parrot something.

If you are feeling especially brave, you may want to hand out a "Teacher Rating Sheet" to your students at the end of the unit. The sheet can consist of several statements to which the students rate from

0 (strongly disagree) to 10 (strongly agree). You may include statements such as:

1) I have learned a lot about [topic] this quarter.

2) The teacher asks questions that are thoughtful and interesting.

3) I usually have no trouble following class discussion.

4) The teacher is organized and well-prepared.

5) I usually leave class knowing how to apply the lesson to my life.

It is also helpful to balance the rated statements with a few fill-in-the-blank statements, such as:

Of the activities, exercises, and discussions we have done in class:

1) The one I found most effective was _____.

2) The one I found least effective was _____.

3) One thing I would have liked to do in class is _____.

4) The biggest strength of my teacher is _____.

5) My teacher needs to improve in the area of _____.

Younger students may not be able to fill out a sheet such as this, but you can interview the class, rewording these statements for young children. You could also ask another teacher to sit in on a class and fill out an evaluation sheet.

Granted, putting yourself through this kind of scrutiny makes you feel very vulnerable, but it pays off. This kind of feedback helps you hone your skills and grow. Try not to let honest criticism discourage you. Some students can be brutal in their feedback and tenacious in their determination (however misdirected it may be) to save you from the sin of pride. Take it in the spirit it is intended. Some people care enough to say the very worst.

## SELF-EVALUATION

You should also jot down your own reaction to your teaching during or immediately after a lesson. Was a particular teaching method wildly successful or a dismal failure? Did the lesson hit a snag at any point? Was the introduction more or less effective than the other parts of the lesson?

When you have compiled a good number of thoughts, compare this to your lesson notes—remember, these are the notes you are supposed to ignore while you are teaching. After the lesson is over, however, you should study them thoroughly. Did you achieve the lesson aim? Did you forget anything? Would the lesson have been better if you had included something else? Did the teaching method(s) work well? How could you do it better the next time?

These notes and your self-evaluation should be the first thing you review when you start preparing for the next lesson. They can help you discover where your teaching needs improvement so that you can work on it, and determine where your strengths are.

It is very important, by the way, to try to avoid a subjective bias in your evaluation. For example, if I don't like to use games as a teaching method, I will tend to be negative in my evaluation of a lesson in which I used a game. But if the students liked it and seemed to learn from it, I need to be more objective.

## OTHER SOURCES

Besides the direct responses of your students and your own class notes, there are other sources of evaluation:

1) *Outside class activities can be a way to tell if your teaching sticks.* Watch your students outside of the classroom. Are they talking about and living the concepts they've learned in class? One lesson on love is not likely to turn a bully into a saint overnight, but if your teaching is having any effect, over time you should be able to see it, however subtle.

2) *In-class review of the previous week's content is another way to see if*

*the lesson is getting through.* If students can remember anything you taught from the previous Sunday after a full and busy week, you are really reaching them!

3) *Testing is a useful evaluation technique because it can help the teacher and the student discover what has been learned.* If you are afraid you may be burned at the stake for daring to give an exam in Sunday school, remember that a simple activity such as a trivia game can be a painless form of testing. Also remember that it must be age-level appropriate. Perhaps with younger children it would be useful to have input from parents to see if the children understand the Bible lessons.

4) A *review session is a helpful evaluation method as well.* It can take the form of a question-and-answer session, buzz groups, or other student discussion methods. Take note of what things the students remember and what they have trouble recalling. Combined with your weekly evaluation notes, a review session can reveal patterns that are not as noticeable on a week-to-week basis.

None of these evaluation methods, however, can eliminate the need to do the hard and often humbling task of self-review. While it's important to find out if your students are learning, your more immediate need is to find out why or why not. If your students remember and can apply the lesson from the previous week, that's wonderful. But why did it work last week but not the week before? What teaching method(s) did you use that were effective? What didn't work and why?

---

**Evaluation is intended to be for your benefit, not your detriment.**

---

Evaluation is intended to be for your benefit, not your detriment. The feedback you get can sometimes be discouraging, but remind yourself that no one is perfect. With healthy and honest evaluation, however, you can expect to see continual improvement.

**THINKING IT OVER:**

1) What are ways you evaluate during class, such as reading students' faces?

2) Have you done evaluation after a class is over? What did you find out about your teaching?

3) Try the techniques suggested in this chapter and use your notes and observations to prepare for a later class. Do you see this to be helpful? How?

**MAKING IT WORK:**

Take the lesson you worked on in previous chapters, and prepare a list of review questions for it. Decide what form of the review these questions lend themselves to, such as a test, a trivia game, a survey, or some other format.

# <u>Notes</u>

# Chapter Nine

# Creating Your Own Curriculum

CHUCK COULD SEE BOB, THE SUNDAY SCHOOL DIRECTOR, ZEROING IN ON HIM AS SOON AS THE MORNING SERVICE ENDED. With a wide grin and an easy manner, Bob wrapped his burly arm around Chuck's shoulders and squeezed. "How's my favorite Sunday school teacher?"

"Not too bad, I guess," Chuck responded, trying not to wince in pain. Bob's heart was in the right place, but he didn't know his own strength. "So, what's up?"

Suddenly, the vice-like grip was gone, and Bob was facing Chuck eye-to-eye, looking dreadfully serious. "I need to ask a favor."

"Go ahead," Chuck replied, remembering Bob's fabled powers of persuasion. Bob could sell water skis in Death Valley.

"I'd like to ask you to take the college and career class this spring. The students are interested in studying that new book on evangelism by Dr. Waldo Beasley. You've heard of him?"

"Oh, yes," Chuck responded. "He's pretty deep but solidly biblical. Now, what's the catch?"

"Catch?"

"C'mon, Bob, don't play games with me. I know you too well. You don't come over here and flash your million-dollar smile just to ask me to teach my favorite age group! There's got to be some catch."

"Chuck, you're so skeptical!" Bob said, laughing. "No, there's no catch, really; I mean, you would have to teach the class without a leader's guide, but—"

"What?!"

"Now, Chuck," Bob assumed a fatherly tone to his voice, and the burly arm clamped down on Chuck's shoulders again. "When they asked me about this class, I thought of you immediately. You've really gotten good at this 'customizing curriculum' thing; creating your own approach for going through this book is just the next logical step."

Chuck pondered the idea; teach without any teacher's guide? "Well, if I did this, would you be willing to help me out?"

"Of course, Chuck—any way I can."

"Good, because I'll be away for two weeks in the middle of the quarter—you could be my substitute!"

---

**While such a class (usually taught as an elective) requires more preparation and creativity, you may find this challenge very exhilarating!**

---

For any number of reasons—a tight budget, dissatisfaction with published curriculum, student requests, or the suggestion of the Sunday school director—you may find yourself being asked to teach without any curriculum at all. While such a class (usually taught as an elective) requires more preparation and creativity, you may find this challenge very exhilarating!

An elective class such as this usually takes the form of an in-depth study on an extended passage of Scripture (often with the assistance of one or more commentaries) or a topical study using a popular Christian book.

## SINGLE-PASSAGE STUDIES

A study that focuses on one book of the Bible or some other extended, self-contained passage can be very exciting to teach because you can focus intently on that particular portion of God's Word. Of course, you would also look at related passages, allowing Scripture to interpret Scripture. But the point of a single-passage study is that it allows the topic under discussion to be determined by the passage and not vice versa. This type of study makes it easier for the Bible to speak to you and your students. The agenda of the class is determined by the Lord and His Word, not by your own interests.

## CHOOSING A PASSAGE

In choosing a portion of Scripture for a weekly study, find one that fits your style of teaching and the interests of the class. Some books of the Bible, such as the New Testament letters, lend themselves to in-depth, verse-by-verse study, while others, such as some of the Old Testament historical books, can be taught in a panoramic overview, often covering multiple chapters in a single lesson.

A study of several related passages, such as the parables of Christ, would also be appropriate for an extended-passage study. Another possibility is character study, such as the missionary journeys of Paul or the life of King David which require extensive research to do well and avoid misinterpretations. A Sunday school elective such as this could more easily be done using a popular book by a reputable author.

Keep in mind the age you are teaching when choosing a passage.

You may find it difficult to teach some books of the Bible to younger students. For example, teens or even preteens may be able to accept the strange behavior recorded in the book of Judges as the result of people doing what was "right in their own eyes"; elementary and upper elementary, however, may have a great deal of trouble understanding the events in that book.

## PLANNING AHEAD FOR SUCCESS

Teaching a Bible study without a curriculum will require advance preparation at the beginning of the course. The following suggestions can help you do it successfully:

1) *Read ahead.* Before the class begins, read and reread the entire book or passage to be covered. Take extensive notes, searching for repeated words, and recurring themes. If you have a Bible with cross-references, jot down some of these passages for further study. Don't, however, attempt an in-depth study at this point; all you want to do is to get a good overview of the material.

2) *Plan your strategy.* Your advance reading should give you an idea of where to divide the material into weekly lessons. Often it is useful to begin the first week's lesson with an introduction to the book or passage and its author. Typically such a Sunday school elective can continue for 11 more weeks, concluding on the thirteenth week with a quarterly review. An introductory week and a review week can be very helpful, but they are optional. Some churches offer different lengths of courses as well: six, eight, or more weeks, etc. Use these time frames to help you plan the study and choose the content.

Look for natural divisions in the biblical text that allow each lesson to be built around a single point or idea—the lesson aim. This means that sometimes the passage under study may not fit neatly into the chapter divisions. Don't worry about it; the chapter divisions don't always provide the best fit for a lesson. In the same way, don't be too concerned if one week's lesson consists of only a half dozen verses while the next week's lesson covers a chapter and a half. This is not important as long as a single point can be taught comprehensively.

*3) Package the course.* Based on your reading, develop a theme for the study and a list of topics that will be covered in the weeks ahead. Try to come up with an interesting, memorable title for the course. The title will help you keep the course theme in mind as you teach and create an atmosphere of excitement and interest which is more conducive to learning. Besides, if it's an elective class, you'll want to attract students!

*4) Compile your resources.* There are a number of lay-level commentaries available on every book of the Bible. Many contain everything from discussion questions to historical and cultural background, and they can be a great help. Remember, however, that the commentary cannot teach for you! You must do the study necessary to have a good command of the passage. (See Appendix A for suggested resources.)

When a teacher fails to plan ahead, a Bible study can get out of control. One extreme example I know of is a teacher who began a study in Genesis without any extended planning but with the enthusiastic cooperation of his students. When the session ended, they were not very far along, so the class continued into the next session—and the next, and the next. After three years the teacher moved out of the area. By then, the class was only in chapter 11, and the students were clamoring to study anything but Genesis!

## WEEKLY BIBLICAL PREPARATION

As you plan out your lesson each week, keep in mind that preparing your own curriculum gives you an added responsibility to maintain a biblical foundation. Make doubly sure that the lesson aim is drawn from the content of the passage being studied and not something you're imposing onto the text. Thorough reading and re-reading of the passage will help you avoid imposing your own ideas into the Scripture. The lesson should be the Bible's content in your style.

---

**Each step builds on the other: the more thoroughly you read a passage, observing its details and subtleties, the easier it will be to interpret what the passage means; the more time you spend in thoughtful meditation about the interpretation of a passage, the clearer you will see its application to life.**

---

The "OIL" acronym from Chapter Two (Observation, Interpretation, Life application) is an important procedure as you prepare for the lesson as well as when you present the lesson. Each step builds on the other: the more thoroughly you read a passage, observing its details and subtleties, the easier it will be to interpret what the passage means; the more time you spend in thoughtful meditation about the interpretation of a passage, the clearer you will see its application to life.

In applying it to life, strive to go beyond the surface. Be careful to resist obvious conclusions or strained moralizing. It is very easy to take a simplistic response to a biblical teaching or to look for a "moral to the story" that may not be supported by the passage. The only protection from this danger is thoughtful, prayerful study of the Word, finding the subtle but central message.

If you have scholarly leanings, take advantage of them. While you should avoid an approach that goes over your students' heads, it is possible to add solid biblical research into a lesson without making it obscure or intimidating. For example, if the meaning of a word in the original Greek is relevant to the discussion, by all means include it— but there is no need to confuse your students by quoting the Greek! Strive to communicate, not to impress.

## TOPICAL STUDIES

What if you want to do a Bible study on a particular topic rather than a specific passage? Topical studies can be fascinating, but unless they are backed by hours of research, they can tend to become little more than a collection of "proof-texts" for each point. You may find it hard to keep the attention of your class with the shallow content of such a study. If you really want to do a Sunday school elective on a particular topic, try using a popular Christian book by a reputable author—someone who has already done the necessary in-depth research.

Many topical Christian books include discussion questions or even a leader's guide which can be very useful. But some good books do not have leader's guides, and both you and your class can often learn a lot more than you would with a teacher's guide. Using the three-point outline (Introduction, Body, and Conclusion), you can customize the book's content into lessons which reflect your own teaching style and the personality of your students (something you may choose to do even if you are using a teacher's guide). And besides, it's a challenge. This type of teaching will keep you on your toes and get your adrenaline pumping. It won't be dull for you and certainly not for your class.

Regardless of whatever helps the book may or may not contain, you can still adapt the weekly lessons to the three-point outline by following steps similar to those used with curriculum:

*1) Read the whole book first.* As you read, try to capture the book's main theme into a sentence or two.

*2) Divide the book into sections for weekly lessons.* Typically, a week's lesson can be a single chapter, but some books may contain long chapters that could be covered over two weeks or short, related chapters that could be combined. (Some books with leader's guides are already divided into lessons to be used specifically as Sunday school electives.)

*3) Boil down each chapter into a separate theme of a sentence or two.* This theme can be the basis of your lesson aim.

*4) Put each chapter and theme at the top of a separate sheet of paper.* Under that, put all the subheads within the chapter and all the Scripture references that are cited in the chapter. Are there any notable anecdotes, pithy statements, or listed points in the chapter? Highlight these in the chapter text, and note them on your sheet.

*5) Do the chapters contain discussion questions at the end?* If so, write these down on the sheet, taking note of questions you may want to eliminate or reword.

With these steps done, you have all the raw materials necessary to prepare the lesson using a three-point outline. These steps can be done week by week as you prepare the lesson, but there are advantages to doing this kind of preliminary work ahead of time. If you prepare your list for each chapter as you read the book, you'll find that you read with one eye open to the details which saves you time and trouble. Besides, you'll get an idea of where you are going with the book—the "big picture."

If each student has a copy of the book and is reading the appropriate chapter prior to class, your goal is not as much to teach new material as it is to reinforce the points of the chapter. Don't be concerned about those who have not read the book; ideally, they will learn a lot even without having read the chapter, and they will see the importance of reading the chapter if they want to participate.

Creating your own curriculum can take a little extra time, but it is an exciting challenge and a spark to your creativity.

## THINKING IT OVER:

1) Which type of study—extended Bible passage or topical Christian book—appeals to you the most? Why?

2) Try using the "OIL" method on a short passage of Scripture. After thorough study of the passage, compare your findings with those of a good lay-level commentary. How do they differ? How are they similar?

3) Compile the "raw material" from one chapter of a topical Christian book. Could you prepare a lesson using a three-point outline from this material? If not, how would you supplement the material?

## MAKING IT WORK:

Choose a topical Christian book or an extended passage of Scripture, and prepare a proposal for a Sunday school elective class at your church. Show the proposal to your Sunday school director, and ask for input on how to improve the proposal.

# Bible Study
# Resources

When you do Bible study preparation for your teaching or you are developing a curriculum without a teacher's guide, these are reference materials that I recommend:

1. A good study Bible, with notes and cross-references, e.g., *NIV Study Bible*, *The Open Bible*, etc.

2. *How to Read the Bible for All Its Worth*. Gordon Fee and Douglas Stuart. Grand Rapids: Zondervan, 1980, 1993.
This is an excellent volume on how to understand and interpret God's Word. There are separate chapters on interpreting different parts of the Bible. This book explains, for example, how you need to look at a poetic passage (such as Psalms) differently than a historical passage (such as Joshua) or a prophetic passage (such as Ezekiel). You can save yourself an amazing amount of frustration and confusion when you stop trying to read the entire Bible as if it were one kind of writing!

3. *The New Strong's Exhaustive Concordance*. James Strong. Nashville: Thomas Nelson, 1995, 1996.

Using this concordance (called exhaustive because it lists every occurrence of every word in the Bible—not because it's so heavy!), you can look up the meaning of specific words in a passage without having to learn Greek or Hebrew. Be sure to read "Instructions to the Reader" in the front of the volume. (This volume is based on the King James Version; there are similar exhaustive concordances with Hebrew and Greek word definitions for other translations.)

4. *Unger's Bible Handbook*. Merrill F. Unger, Chicago: Moody, 1966.

This handy little book is a commentary on every book of the Bible, along with maps, charts, historical background information, and other valuable material. It provides lots of information at an affordable price.

5. Lay Person Commentaries: *The Zondervan NIV Bible Commentary*. Grand Rapids: Zondervan, 1994.

This commentary comes in two massive volumes, one for the Old Testament and one for the New Testament. It is thorough and detailed but doesn't get overly technical or academic.

6. God's Word for the Biblically-Inept series, from Starburst Publishers, is a lot of fun to read, and it includes quite a bit of background information in a very popular format. One book in the series is a commentary on the entire Bible; others in the series cover individual books of the Bible.

7. The Everyman's Bible Commentary series, from Moody Press, consists of inexpensive paperback volumes for individual books of the Bible. They are very informative and readable.

8. *"Be" Series*. Warren W. Wiersbe, Colorado Springs: Cook
    Communications Ministries.
Dr. Wiersbe is Writer-in-Residence at Cornerstone College in Grand Rapids, Michigan, and Distinguished Professor of Preaching at Grand Rapids Baptist Seminary. He has pastored three churches, including Moody Church in Chicago, and served as General Director and Bible teacher for Back to the Bible Broadcast. This series of books covers every Book in the Bible and includes a personal and group study guide. For more information, you can access the web site at www.cookministries.com.

9. *Home Bible Study Library*. Lawrence O. Richards. Colorado
    Springs: Cook Communications Ministries.
The *Home Bible Study Library* is designed to help you be more knowledgeable and effective in your ministry. It is comprised of four volumes: *Bible Teacher's Commentary*, *Devotional Commentary*, *Bible Reader's Companion*, and *New Testament Life and Times*. Written by Dr. Larry Richards—renowned Bible scholar, educator, and master communicator—these helpful works are clear, insightful, and practical.

10. *The Bible Exposition Commentary*. Warren W. Wiersbe.
    Colorado Springs: Cook Communications Ministries.
Compiled from Dr. Wiersbe's best-selling "Be" series. Four volumes are currently available: Old Testament (Genesis—

Deuteronomy), Old Testament and the Prophets, New Testament Volume 1, and New Testament Volume 2. Other books are due to be added to this series.

11. *The Bible Knowledge Commentary*. John F. Walvoord and Roy B. Zuck. Colorado Springs: Cook Communications Ministries.

This commentary comes in two large volumes, Old Testament and New Testament.

# Teaching Methods

The following general categories of teaching methods should give you an idea as to what will work best for you in your particular situation. The examples in parentheses after each category are far from exhaustive, but they may help jump-start your imagination.

**LECTURE**
(Sermon, monologue, storytelling, demonstration, symposium)

*Age Range:* All ages; adjust to attention span.

*Advantages:* Good for presenting a lot of content in the least amount of time, in a structured and systematized way; works well with other methods and in large classes.

*Disadvantages:* Low student participation can lead to boredom; lack of feedback stifles students' initiative; not all teachers are skilled public speakers.

*Tips for Use:* Prepare and outline well; use examples and illustrations; avoid jargon, and speak in a conversational manner; supplement with visual aids and other methods.

## DISCUSSION
(Buzz groups, debate, forum, problem solving, case study, question-answer)

*Age Range:* 3rd or 4th grade to adult.

*Advantages:* High student participation increases interest and forces students to think, listen, and express ideas; helps teacher discover students' needs and errors in thinking.

*Disadvantages:* Potential "pooling of ignorance"; can be time-consuming; conversation can lag, get sidetracked or monopolized by one or two people; teacher needs to maintain control without stifling lively discussion; can be less effective in larger groups.

*Tips for Use:* Prepare and outline topic well; set time limits and announce them; break up a large class into smaller groups; seat students in a circle or semi-circle.

## ART/CRAFT
(Drawing, painting, charts and graphs, posters, sculpture, crafts)

*Age Range:* All ages; tends to face more resistance with older students.

*Advantages:* High student participation; high "fun" factor;

especially attractive to visual learners and kinesthetic learners.

*Disadvantages:* Can have low content; may be frustrating for students lacking aptitude in this area and boring for artistic students; can be time-consuming and messy.

*Tips for Use:* Merge with more content-laden method; choose projects that are simple to do but which provide an opportunity to be creative in fine details; continue complex projects over multiple class sessions.

## READING
(Inductive Bible study, research projects, magazine articles, handouts)

*Age Range:* 3rd or 4th grade to adult.

*Advantages:* Good for presenting a lot of content in a structured and systematized way; works well with other methods and in large classes.

*Disadvantages:* May be frustrating for students lacking aptitude or boring for more academic students; can be time-consuming; limited interaction with other students.

*Tips for Use:* Carefully choose reading materials and projects that are appropriate to the age/educational level of students; keep material short, or save a portion of it for a homework assignment; merge with discussion or other method; ask for volunteers to read aloud rather than "assigning" verses or sections randomly.

## WRITING
(Essays, tests, written prayers, poems, stories and parables, Bible paraphrase)

*Age Range:* 3rd or 4th grade to adult.

*Advantages:* Can be high in content and structured; offers opportunity for student self-expression; can give teacher needed feedback; works well with other methods.

*Disadvantages:* Teacher needs great tact in pointing out students' errors in content; writing may be frustrating for students lacking aptitude or boring for more academic or creative students; can be time-consuming; limited interaction with other students.

*Tips for Use:* Make writing assignments well-defined; avoid setting a required length; set a specific time for completion, but allow students who are not done to finish it at home; merge with other methods or have students work in teams.

## MUSIC
(Singing, songwriting, analyzing lyrics, hymn paraphrasing)

*Age Range:* All ages; may have limited value with older students.

*Advantages:* High student participation; high "fun" factor; may reach music lovers on a deeper level than any other method; works well with other methods.

*Disadvantages:* Varying musical tastes in the class can make choosing music difficult; the content (especially the doctrinal perspective) of lyrics can vary in quality; varying musical skill and knowledge of students can lead to frustration or boredom.

*Tips for Use:* Get feedback from the class on their tastes in music; look for recorded music that includes written devotional material; merge with other methods or have students work in teams (preferably pairing the more musically-oriented students with those who are less comfortable with this method).

## DRAMA
(Skits, pantomime, puppets, roleplay, fictional interview)

*Age Range:* All ages; limited value with older students.

*Advantages:* High student participation; high "fun" factor; can be especially useful to help students apply lesson concepts; works well with other methods.

*Disadvantages:* Some students may be shy about participating; can be time-consuming; "ad-libbing" and "hamming it up" by students can get the lesson off-track.

*Tips for Use:* Make participation optional (somebody has to be the "audience"!); keep the "script" or activity short and to the point; keep a short leash on budding thespians.

## GAME
(Bible quizzing, contests, "trivia" quizzes, competitions, board games)

*Age Range:* All ages; limited value with older students.

*Advantages:* High content, high student participation, high "fun" factor, works well with other methods.

*Disadvantages:* Can be time-consuming; may be a danger of appearing to "trivialize" content

*Tips for Use:* Incorporate the lesson content into a well-known parlor game or game-show format, to save the time usually spent explaining rules; present the content of the lesson with more "serious" methods, and use games to reinforce earlier teaching; be sensitive to students who have not been in class or are new when setting up competition.

## MIXING METHODS

Some methods appeal to only one or two types of learners. By combining methods, you can reach more students at the same time. Besides, mixing methods is a lot of fun. Here are some examples of how you can combine two methods into one or use two methods simultaneously:

- Combine lecture with drama and do a dramatic monologue, such as retelling a Bible story as an eyewitness. Get into the spirit by presenting your monolgue in costume.

- Combine lecture and discussion to create a question-and-answer session, or have lecture followed by discussion as a response to the lecture content.

- Begin with buzz groups discussing a topic or Scripture passage; then conclude with an art project that can be done as a group, such as a mural that ties in your discussion about the Scripture.

- Combine lecture and reading by providing a handout with the main points of the material about which you are speaking. Your lecture should not be a straight reading of the written material but rather an expansion and clarification of the written points.

- Combine music with writing by playing an appropriate hymn or popular song and having the students write down what they learn from the music about the lesson topic.

- Combine buzz groups with research by assigning each group a passage to study and report on to the rest of the class.

- Combine Bible study with class discussion by having everyone read and take notes on a passage individually, and then discuss it as a group.

- Lecture, writing, and a game can be put together by speaking on the topic of the lesson as the students write down answers to a list of questions. The individual or team that answers the most questions correctly wins the game.

- Combine art with Bible study by having students illustrate an event in Scripture or outline the route of a biblical traveler (the Israelites leaving Egypt or Paul's missionary journeys) on a map.

See how easy it is? Start your mental gears turning, and come up with a few combinations of your own. Some of the best teaching occurs when you combine audience methods (such as lecture) with participant methods (such as discussion), and individual methods (such as writing) with group activities (such as a game). So let your creativity take off!

# Notes

**INTRODUCTION**
1) "Roger's Story." This true story is used by permission of Pastor Dan Betzer of Florida.

**CHAPTER 2 — WHERE DO YOU FIT IN?**
1) Joe D. Marlow, "Analyzing the Curriculum Debate," *Christian Education Journal* (Spring 1993), p. 100.
2) C. Doug Bryan, *Learning to Teach, Teaching to Learn* (Nashville: Broadman and Holman, 1993), p. 91.
3) Marlene LeFever, *Learning Styles: Reaching Everyone God Gave You to Teach* (Colorado Springs: David C. Cook, 1995), p. 25.

**CHAPTER 3 — CUSTOMIZING THE CURRICULUM**
1) Gary Dean, *Handbook of Young Adult Religious Education*, Harley Atkinson, ed. (Birmingham, Ala.: Religious Education Press, 1995), p. 180.

2) John H. Walton, Laurie D. Bailey and Craig Williford, "Bible-based Curricula and the Crisis of Scriptural Authority," *Christian Education Journal* (Spring 1993), pp. 83, 85.

3) Marlene LeFever, *Learning Styles: Reaching Everyone God Gave You to Teach* (Colorado Springs, Colo.: David C. Cook, 1995).


CHAPTER 4 — RIGHTLY DIVIDING THE WORD

1) Paul Little, *Who Said That?* comp. George Sweeting (Chicago: Moody, 1994, 1995), p. 69.

2) *Who Said That?* comp. George Sweeting (Chicago: Moody, 1994, 1995), p. 70.

3) John H. Walton, Laurie D. Bailey and Craig Williford, "Bible-based Curricula and the Crisis of Scriptural Authority," *Christian Education Journal* (Spring 1993), p. 88.


CHAPTER 5 — HOOKS TO HANG TRUTH ON

1) Marlene LeFever, *Learning Styles: Reaching Everyone God Gave You to Teach* (Colorado Springs, Colo.: David C. Cook, 1995), pp. 99-107.

2) *The Alliance World*, (Fall 1995), pp. 42-43.


CHAPTER 6 — THE WORDS OF YOUR MOUTH

1) Augustine, "On the Catechizing of the Uninitiated," as cited by Luther Allan Weigle, *Talks to Sunday School Teachers* (New York: George H. Doran Co., 1920), p. 121.

2) *Who Said That?* comp. George Sweeting (Chicago: Moody, 1995), p. 295.

3) *The Alliance World*, (Summer 1998), pp. 29-30.

## CHAPTER 7— IT'S SHOW TIME!

1) William M. Timpson, et al., *Teaching and Performing* (Madison, Wis.: Magna Publications, 1997).

2) Luther Allan Weigle, *Talks to Sunday School Teachers* (New York: George H. Doran Co., 1920), p. 107.

3) Mavis Weidman, ed., *Charting the Course* (Harrisburg, PA: Christian Publications, 1955), p. 53.s